David Cooper lives in Glencoe where he runs the family business Crafts & Things, and actively pursues his interests of sailing, photography and listening to live music.

D1152267

A Gap Life

DAVID COOPER

Suilven Press

First published in 2016 by Suilven Press
Crafts & Things, Glencoe PH49 4HN.
www.craftsandthings.co.uk

ISBN: 978-0-9927233-4-7

Printed in the UK by Bell & Bain Ltd., Glasgow.

The paper used in this book is recyclable. It is made from low
chlorine pulps produced in a low energy, low emissions manner
from renewable forests.

Typeset and design by Main Point Books,
77 Bread Street, Edinburgh EH3 9AH.
www.mainpointbooks.co.uk

Contents

Heaven and Earth are only a few feet apart.
In the thin places, that distance is even smaller.
(Celtic saying)

We are all, to a large extent, just an expression of our experiences. Here, for the benefit of my two sons, are mine, in the hope that they will understand who I am and forgive me a little. This book is dedicated to the memory of my brother Robin.

David Cooper, Glencoe, June 2016

CHAPTER ONE

Early Days

'So you are off to Australia for how long? Two years did you
say? A double gap year!'
'Well you can't talk Dad, you are having a gap life!'

I am not sure about reincarnation but I like the idea of my
soul hovering around the sacred Hebridean island of Iona in
the summer of 1949. My parents, Tony and Ursula enjoyed
holidays there, camping above the soft white sands of Port Ban
on the west side of the island, itself perched off the westernmost
tip of Mull. According to the theory, the soul enters the body at
the time of conception, and having with them my elder brother
Robin and sister Jo, aged five and seven respectively, time to
themselves would have been precious, but time they found and
I was born in March 1950, at home, just outside Tarland in
Aberdeenshire.

John Anthony Cooper, Tony to his friends, was a complex
man. Over his long life he had been a jack of all trades, master
of none. He was born and grew up in Chorley Wood, London
in 1911. He lived in Cheshire for a while, playing rugby for the
county, competing at a regional level against, on one occasion,
the national New Zealand side, the All Blacks. He was studying
at a university in Germany when the looming war forced an

early return home. He enlisted and became a captain in charge of a coastal gun defence battery in Kent. His location was the first to have radar installed and after this was discovered by German intelligence, his position was heavily bombed. These attacks and the constant noise of his own battery of guns firing at incoming German aircraft and the flying 'doodlebug' bomb were more than his nervous system could take, and he was hospitalised for several months. He never talked about this breakdown or any of his other wartime experiences, no doubt feeling stigmatised and ashamed.

Tony was close to his mother and when she died whilst he was still a teenager, he was devastated. She was musically talented and sang on occasions in the Albert Hall. No doubt she inspired his love of music and he played the piano and cello until arthritis and deafness took their toll.

During the war Tony met his wife, Ursula Talbot. She was working in the Bank of England alongside her father, a veteran of World War One, who had survived the war in a spotter balloon directing allied shells onto enemy targets. She recalled a morning soon after she had turned three, being dressed up in her finest clothes and told to wait until this man, a complete stranger to her, walked into the house she shared with her mother. 'Say hello to your father,' she was told, 'he is back from the war and will be living here now.' For some reason she named him 'Pom-Pom.' The name stuck and that was how I knew him throughout his life.

Soon after the outbreak of the Second World War, she accepted an invitation to a dance from a dapper young soldier who introduced her to his brother Tony, with whom she left the dance. Quite what this did for sibling relations I do not know but in later years the brothers were to argue and go their separate ways, a split never reconciled.

Tony and Ursula made a handsome couple. He in his Number

One uniform, standing tall and proud, was an athletic, solidly built man with a burgeoning moustache that in time was to spread over his face to create an impressive set of whiskers. She was tall, elegant and from the available photos, a striking-looking woman. They married in 1941.

Ursula was an only child and, having no siblings, grew up preferring the company of animals, especially dogs, to that of people. She was proud of her family heritage, which she could trace back to the 1760s and the Fourth Marquis of Lothian, via a couple of army generals and, closer to her, the Eden family which included the former Prime Minister Sir Anthony, whose leading role in the disastrous Suez crisis in 1956 caused his resignation the following year. She spent many childhood holidays with her Eden cousins in Yorkshire and the south-west of England, memorable days which she was able to recall in detail well into her nineties.

Tony and Ursula lived in Basingstoke, where on New Year's Day 1943 the first of their four children was born. Jocelyn Elizabeth, 'Jo' as she became known, was a bright, bouncing baby girl who soon developed a head of long, curly blonde hair. Bringing up a child in wartime would have been challenging, with food shortages and enemy attacks to cope with. Ursula and her daughter had a couple of narrow escapes. A low flying Messerschmitt, appearing out of nowhere with its machine guns blazing, bullets spewing up the grass beside the pram, must have been terrifying. And later, having been caught outside in an air raid, a bomb landing a few yards away failed to explode. Subsequent examination revealed that it had been filled with sawdust in a German munitions factory by an allied sympathiser, to whom I owe my life.

After the war ended, Tony moved his family north of the border to Scotland. Something about the quality and pace of life attracted them, along with the opportunities he hoped would present themselves to someone with no formal qualifications but with a strong work ethic. They initially settled in Edinburgh where their second child, my brother Robin, was born at Elsie Inglis hospital in April 1945.

For a short spell Tony found work away from home near Cupar in Fife. Reading his letters to Ursula in Edinburgh, it is clear he was desperate to find secure employment and a house for his expanding family. He started with a large agricultural company called Bibby's, which bought grain from farmers and sold them the equipment they needed to harvest it. Eventually he was given a sales area of his own, the lucrative, farm-wealthy Aberdeenshire, and in 1947 he bought Loch Coull House, just outside Tarland, a few miles from Aboyne. It was a large, rambling, south-facing building in its own grounds surrounded by tall pine trees, a two-tiered front garden with magnificent views over the moorlands of West Aberdeenshire and a long access drive. I can only assume that the death of his parents had left Tony some capital to finance the purchase.

Their third child, Timothy, died within twenty-four hours of his birth. Ursula would tell us in later years the harrowing account of lying in a hospital bed having given birth a few hours earlier and listening to a baby crying. She knew the baby was hers but she had not been allowed to hold or comfort him; his cries got weaker throughout the night, eventually stopping around dawn. Fortunately, the trauma of this experience did not put them off having me, their fourth child.

Life must have been good for the young Cooper family in those early post-war years. Tony worked hard, exceeding targets, winning accolades and prizes from his employers and bringing in a steady income. He was able to develop his hobbies: beekeeping, painting, gardening, fishing, and playing the cello and piano. His beloved black and white collie, Mickey, was never far from his side and together they would set off on long walks in the early morning over the moorlands.

The mist lay low over the land one morning when Tony was surprised to see a rider on horseback looming out of the mirk – he was used to having the moors to himself at this early hour. Turning his horse, the man rode over to Tony, dismounted, took off his hat and greeted him with a firm handshake. They chatted for a good half hour, about the weather, farming and the local wildlife, making banal conversation and sharing a joke or two, before the stranger looked at his watch.

'They will be looking for me, I had better head back,' he said as he swung back onto the saddle. 'It's been a real pleasure chatting to you: I hope we can do this again.'

'I hope so too,' Tony replied, 'God speed.'

The horseman rode away, disappearing into the mist. Tony had recognised him immediately, but decided that the man would probably enjoy a conversation with one of his subjects without the formality his position would normally command. It was King George the Sixth.

Tony and Ursula slotted into local society life, entertaining and being entertained, and occasionally being invited to society balls. They had a handyman to help about the property, a German ex-POW called Klaus, who had decided to stay in Scotland after the war and had married a local girl; he remained in the area for the rest of his life. They also employed a nanny, though her time with the family was short-lived after she dropped me on the floor when I was just a few days old. Jo and Robin started primary school at the nearby village of Coull, learning to write with chalk on slate. The winters could be harsh; access to the house cut off with snow, which would cover the telegraph poles. January 1953 was particularly bad and Ursula decided she needed a break away from the weather to visit family friends who were in the Army, stationed in Coleraine, Northern Ireland. She booked a passage on a boat for herself and me, due to leave

Stranraer on January 31st, but the forecast was dreadful and at the last moment she decided to fly instead. The boat left the harbour that morning without us. The *Princess Victoria*, one of the first roll-on/roll-off car ferries, was soon out of the shelter of Loch Ryan and facing gale-force winds. The stern doors broke; the ship was flooded and sank. One hundred and thirty-three lives were lost that day, and of the forty survivors, there were no women or children.

But mostly our family holidays were on Iona.

'Wake up, wake up, it's time to get up.' My mother was standing over my little bed and I knew something was not right. It was summer, and still dark. It felt as though I had only just gone to sleep, and I was grumpy. Tony was up and about, Jo and Robin were getting dressed, and there was a buzz of excitement about the place. I had no idea why. Tony appeared with porridge for us, served up in the wooden bowls he had turned on his lathe. Unusually for me, food was the last thing on my mind, but we ate breakfast in a hurry, and still half-asleep were bundled into the old black Austin which Tony had to hand crank to start, and then we were off. The sun had still not risen by the time we reached the Devil's Elbow, the notorious double hairpin bend on a steep incline on the main road south-west. Despite the empty roads, progress was slow, but we had a schedule to keep. We had to catch the MacBrayne ferry from Oban, which left promptly at midday on its daily circumnavigation of the island of Mull; Tarland to Oban in that car and on those roads was an arduous undertaking.

In all the times we made the journey, we never once missed the ferry. There was the occasional close call. Once, Tony had to climb up to the ship's bridge to request a delay in departure whilst my mother went off for some essential supplies from Woolworths on Oban's main street. The captain duly obliged, and after much blowing of the horn to get her to hurry up, we sailed only fifteen minutes late.

We were not, however, on a day trip round Mull. TS King George V was a pioneering Clyde-built passenger turbine steamer which in its daily circumnavigation of the island, dropped anchor in the Sound of Iona, opposite the Abbey. Anybody heading for the island could decant into one of the small boats which came out to meet the steamer. This was a perilous process at which a modern-day health and safety officer would throw up their hands in disbelief and despair. Once anchored in the Sound, a door would be removed from the side of the ship, leaving a gaping hole through which one could see the island where we were heading. With a turbulent sea, you would be staring up into the sky one second and into the ocean the next, with a flashing glimpse of Iona in between. The open wooden red boats, each with a small inboard engine, would soon make a welcome appearance underneath the hole left by the removal of the door, and rope netting would be thrown down the side of the ship just reaching the sea. Holding these boats in position were the crew, Big Dougie and Captain Maclean, swarthy Iona men whose legendary boat handling skills were vital for passenger safety. If the King George took a hit from a wave on one side and the red boat go the other way, it would be crushed against the enormous steel hull. These men prevented this from happening.

Anyone coming off the island was encouraged to climb onto the rope netting, like a marine training exercise at an army assault course, and with a push from below and a pull from above, hauled onto the steamer. Then it was time to offload the island provisions and mail onto the constantly moving red boat. Tony had packed our camping gear – beds, ex-army tents, clothes, cooking equipment, food – into an assortment of dark green canvas army bags he had managed to purloin from his days as a soldier. These were unceremoniously thrown into the boat, followed by the dog, then the family, youngest first.

Somehow this went off without a hitch and we arrived on the Iona slipway dry and unharmed.

All my early summers were spent wild camping on Iona. We alternated spots between the machair above Port Ban on the west side, and Sandeels Bay on the east, where the arrival of a puffer caused much activity on the island. The steam-driven, flat-bottomed boat would beach itself at high tide, and, as the tide receded, the islanders would descend to unload the cargo, often the winter's supply of coal, which would be piled high on the beach and divided up amongst its owners before being removed by horse and cart from the fast approaching tide. In the morning the puffer was gone.

Jo, Robin and I were left to our own devices. Iona is not a big island, but once we managed to get hopelessly lost and it took a search party made up of locals and holidaymakers to find us tearfully trying to find our way back to our base.

The camp itself consisted of two large canvas tents, erected with open facing gable ends and a connecting ridge pole, over which a third canvas awning was placed, creating a central communal open eating and cooking space. Meals were prepared over hissing primus stoves, Tony making the porridge in the morning, Ursula taking over for the rest of the meals. We children slept on hay-filled palliasses on top of army camp beds in one tent. The last sound I would hear every night was Tony checking the tent guy rope tensions, hammering in any loose pegs and striking matches to light his pipe for a last smoke before, literally, hitting the hay. Those seemingly endless days of summer were spent gathering driftwood for the fire, collecting drinking water from a slow drip down a small rockface a twenty-minute walk away, searching for cowrie shells, building rafts, paddling in the sea and investigating the contents of every rock pool we could find.

Once we were joined by my father's two brothers, David, after whom I was named, and Jim. Something happened between the brothers on that holiday which prompted a split which proved irreconcilable. Jim and David moved back to South Africa where they had been living. They became almost mythical figures in the family, never talked about: a taboo subject as far as my father was concerned. I only found out about their existence when I was much older, looking at black and white photographs of those Iona holidays.

Many years later, long after Tony had died, I was browsing the internet and stumbled across a writer's blog entitled 'D is for David Cooper'. The author turned out to be a cousin hitherto unknown to me, a female writer living in Germany who was describing her mysterious grandfather, my uncle, who had lived and died in South Africa. She told a sad story about a man who had married her grandmother, had a son and a daughter, and when war broke out enlisted in the South African Desert Rat Corps. She described a cultured man, a charmer, gregarious, handsome and amusing, always well dressed, and artistic, playing the piano, singing, and painting all to a high standard. The war changed all that. He returned from the fighting if not a broken soul, but far removed from the person he was. He sold everything and returned to the UK, but after the fall-out with my father, perhaps over money or an inheritance, returned to South Africa, sad and disillusioned. Divorce soon followed. He eventually remarried, this time to his secretary who also became his guide when cataracts destroyed his sight. The two were sitting together on a park bench in Plettenburg Bay when he suddenly slipped to the ground and died. He was sixty-four.

Back on Iona, Tony and Ursula befriended George MacLeod, later to become the Very Rev. Lord MacLeod of Fuinary, who, with his team of Govan labourers was rebuilding Iona Abbey. Although older than my father, George became a lifelong friend to me, a relationship which started with him christening me in the Abbey in 1950 and ended with his death in 1991, aged ninety-six. The story of George MacLeod and Iona are inextricably linked and is the subject of several books, plays and documentaries. My auspicious start to a potential life of Christian faith did not however materialise. 'The Christening just did not take,' George said to me in later years, after I was heavily committed to an Indian-based meditation exercise. He exemplified the extraordinary power of faith and its ability to overcome all obstacles. In my mid-twenties, he and I sat together in his run-down manse at Fuinary, drams in hand, the setting summer sun streaming through the window, lighting up his face as he described to me some of the now well-documented stories about the rebuilding of the Abbey. These tales rolled off his tongue, his sonorous voice captivating, entrancing, profoundly moving and unforgettable.

'To build you need an ample supply of fresh water, and we had been refused permission by the Duke of Argyll to pipe water across the island. We had a major crisis before one brick had been laid upon another, and it seemed that the entire project would be scuppered before it began. We even brought over water diviners, but that turned out to be a fruitless task. With a heavy heart I instructed the advance party to pack up and get the next steamer home. The workforce had gathered in the Abbey grounds, the steamer was delayed, and as much as to offset boredom as anything else, some started digging around the base of an old tower. They found a well, which was to provide all the water they would ever need.'

The evening shadows grew longer. I sat enthralled. George sipped his dram, and continued.

'During the war, there was an acute shortage of building materials. We could manage for stone, but wood was becoming a problem, and once again we were faced with the situation of having to stop what we were doing because of the lack of available timber. Hundreds of miles away, a ship on passage from Canada to Sweden got into difficulties in a storm. To save his vessel the captain ordered the jettisoning of its deck cargo, which floated all the way down the west coast of Scotland, eventually being washed up on the shore on the coast of Mull, directly opposite the Abbey. The cargo was timber, just the right quantity and length we need to continue the work.'

The last rays of the setting sun silhouetted his large frame, leaving the rest of the room in semi-darkness. But George seemed to be shining with an inner light. These stories were sending shivers down my spine, but he had not finished yet. Clearly enjoying the effect he was having on his single audience, he started up again.

'The cross I wanted for the Abbey had to be very special. I had the image of a piece in silver, large, Celtic, and exquisite.' George and his colleagues had heard of a retrospective exhibition of the work of one of the great British silversmiths, and they travelled together to London to see the exhibits in the hope of finding something suitable for the Abbey altar.

'There was plenty to look at, that was for sure,' he said, 'but one piece stood out from the rest. It was exactly what we were after, just the perfect piece.' The silversmith's widow was there, and they approached her to ask about the magnificent silver cross.

'I am so sorry,' she said, 'but that piece is not for sale. It was one of the last pieces my husband made before he died. It is one he thought was his best work, and he instructed me never to sell it. For one day, he had told her, men will come from Iona, and it is to go there…'

'If you think these are coincidences,' said George, 'then you must lead a very boring life.'

One last incident is less well-known as it was only witnessed by two people. It happened about a week after I had been listening to his Iona stories. We were still at Fuinary Manse, overlooking the Sound of Mull. In the interim, a group of twelve young men from a Young Offenders Institution, or Borstal as it was then called, had arrived for a two-week residence. George had roped me in to help. It fitted in well with placement needs in my social work training, and he was also keen that I should talk to these young offenders about meditation. The lads came with an array of prison staff, and George had also organised a housekeeper called Ann to help out.

One evening, Ann failed to appear for dinner. Eating together was a rule of the house, and I was sent up to her room to fetch her down. I knocked on her door. No reply. Knocked again, 'Ann, are you OK?' I could hear muffled sobs from inside. Clearly something was amiss. 'I am coming in,' I said and slowly opened the door. Ann was sitting on her bed, head in her hands sobbing. 'What on earth is the matter?' I asked.

'I have gone blind!' she cried. She went on to explain that her eyesight had always been bad, and her optician warned her that one day she could lose her sight altogether and that this could happen suddenly. She had been sitting in her room all afternoon and was in desperation. I felt out of my depth. 'I'll go and get George,' I said. 'Back in a minute.'

George and I went back into her room, shut the door, and listened to Ann's story. When she finished, he asked us to kneel down and for me to put my hands on her head. He then laid his hands on top of mine and said 'Jesus, you healed in your lifetime, you are alive and present here, and I demand in your name that you heal this woman and restore her sight.' The effect was immediate. 'Oh my God!' Ann exclaimed, 'I can see!' George then made us both promise not to discuss what had just happened or to reveal it to anyone in his lifetime. The last thing he needed was for his already difficult relationship with Church authorities to be further complicated by stories like this.

But I'm getting ahead of myself. Those early childhood days in Aberdeenshire and Iona came to an end in 1954 when a large green pantechnicon with 'Love's Removals' written along the side arrived to pack up the contents of the house. We were moving to Crieff.

CHAPTER TWO

The Crieff Years

'Get aff the grass!' the angry old man yelled at me. 'Get aff, an'
if I sees ye on it agin I'll skelp ye!'

I was not quite sure what that meant but I could tell from his
tone that it would not be fun, and I scarpered. We had moved
to a cottage with a garden which fronted onto Miller Street, at
the back overlooking a bowling green. I thought I was in heaven
with this large expanse of well-tended grass to kick a ball about
on, but I soon knew better. The 'Bowling Green Man' became
my Bogey Man.

We soon moved into a large mansion that had been subdivided
into four residences, each with a private garden. Adjacent to
the golf course, the area was quietly residential. Our elderly
neighbours, the Wilsons, had invested in a television, then still
something of a novelty. They would invite me in to watch *The
Lone Ranger* or *Champion the Wonder Horse* on a tiny screen
contained in a huge box, a screen which would take fifteen
minutes to warm up before a fuzzy grainy image would appear
– colour TV had yet to be invented. On the other side were
the Ainslies, whose son was my age and a pal until they left to
live in Ireland. And in front were the McGregors. They had a
dog called Barkis which our dog, Donnie, hated. A black and
white collie labrador mix, Donnie was wonderful with people,

but disliked most other dogs. His animosity for Barkis was something special and he would tear lumps out of him at every opportunity. In later years the McGregors' grandson Ewan rose to fame as an actor.

My maternal grandparents also moved to Crieff and took up residence in Burrell Street, one of the busy access roads to the town. Having long retired, they wanted to be near their only child and her family.

Crieff was to be our home for the next sixteen years.

Tony had uprooted the family looking to provide a better education than he imagined would be available in rural Aberdeenshire. My sister Jo was to start at St Margaret's, an Edinburgh girls' school which had relocated during the Second World War to nearby Auchterarder and was yet to move back. Robin and I were destined for Morrison's Academy for Boys.

Being five years older than me, Robin went straight into primary one. I had a few years to wait, before starting kindergarten at Newstead, and then the nursery school, Croftweit, before entering the main school. In my pre-school years my mother would wake me up after my afternoon nap and switch on the wireless for *Listen with Mother*. Meanwhile, Jo was encouraging me to learn to read. Helen Bannerman's *Little Black Sambo* and Heinrich Hoffman's *The Dreadful Story of Harriet and the Matches* were my rather disturbing favourites. I remember Little Black Sambo ended up being chased around a palm tree by a lion until they both turned into butter and were made into pancakes; while the incautious Harriet, who wouldn't take a telling, played with matches and burned the house down.

During my time at Croftweit I developed a stammer and then a lazy eye. The stammer soon disappeared but the squint was more problematic. The first attempts to cure this involved wearing a pink perforated patch over my good eye to strengthen the muscles in the bad. This did not work and an operation became necessary.

When I was deposited at the nearest hospital, sixteen miles away in Perth, I had no idea why I was there or what was going to happen to me. No doubt someone had tried to explain what was going on, but not in a way a six-year-old could understand. I was placed in a large children's ward. Unlike me, everyone else had visitors during the strictly maintained visiting hours. My sense of abandonment was intense. I watched as kids were wheeled out on their beds, to be returned a few hours later, swathed in bandages and, when conscious, crying in pain.

On the third day a nurse came to tell me that it was my turn. My turn to be wheeled out to the unknown, and return a bandaged wreck. A nurse came and covered up one of my eyes; the other was circled with red marker, exposed and ready for the surgeon's knife.

I was told to go to sleep.

I tried my best and when at last men in white coats arrived to wheel me away I kept my eyes tight shut. We travelled down what seemed like miles of corridors. Occasionally I took a peek, trying to take stock of where I was without anyone seeing that I had not obeyed the instruction to fall asleep. Eventually we entered the operating theatre. I could hear different voices and felt the bustle of activity around my bed. I was lifted and put onto a hard surface. Despite the brightest of lights I still pretended to be asleep. Then I had the terrible idea that if they thought I was sleeping they might start to operate. This was too much, and I shot upright, opened my eyes and said loudly and clearly, so that there could be no misunderstanding, 'I am awake!'

The surgeon, who I recognised as someone who had been at my bedside the day before, reassured me. But in sitting up I had knocked over my case notes, which had been placed on my chest. The doctor picked them up, glanced at them, took a longer look, and checked my bandaged face.

'Nurse,' he called, 'you have prepared the wrong eye.'

The bandages were swapped over, and the correct eye successfully operated on.

Three weeks later I was back in Perth Royal Infirmary, this time to have my tonsils removed. At least I knew what to expect. Again I did not see my parents until three days after the operation, but I had learned not to anticipate their visit. The straightforward procedure had not gone to plan, as my adenoids had also been removed, and my nose bled profusely for the next twenty-four hours. I was on the verge of receiving some more blood to top me up when eventually the bleeding stopped. It was Easter, and the local Woolworths had arranged a party for those stuck in hospital on Easter Sunday. The children's ward was bedecked with balloons and streamers, there was a conjuror booked, and the store manager was coming around with an Easter egg for every child. I could not contain my excitement. Some fun in my life, at last.

'When's it starting, when's it starting?' was our constant cry.

'Two o'clock,' the nurses told us.

At half past one my parents turned up to take me home. I was never so disappointed to see them.

At the time, Morrison's Academy was a grant-aided school which accepted both day boys and boarders. Although the girls' school was beside the boys', it was single-sex education, with the access laid out in such a way as to minimise contact between the boys and girls. Passing the eleven plus exam resulted in a free education for the duration of my schooldays. Set in a leafy part of town, with wonderful views over the Perthshire hills, the school building was surrounded by trees and extensive grassland. The outbuildings included a gym, swimming pool, rifle range, sanatorium, a cricket pitch and tennis courts. The extensive rugby and athletics grounds with superb facilities were located a short walk away. Attending the school, as we were constantly reminded, meant we were experiencing a privileged education. And in many ways we were. But on occasion what happened inside those walls was appalling, and would nowadays be regarded as criminal.

There were some dedicated, inspirational teachers. And then there were the others. The History teacher, for instance. His technique was to spend the entire lesson getting us to read aloud from the textbook. Without warning, he would shout out a pupil's name, and that boy had to carry on immediately where the last had stopped. After forty minutes of this on a hot summer afternoon, it was all too easy to lose concentration, and start to daydream.

'Cooper!' The teacher's voice would ring out and my heart would sink. I was not sure what page we were on, let alone what sentence. This was not helped by the person in the seat behind whispering, 'Page forty-five at the top,' or whatever – you never knew if this information could be trusted. And of course if you did not know your place in the book, you were belted.

English was by far my favourite subject. We had no television in the house until I was well into my teens, and I read everything I could lay my hands on, making the three mile round trip to the town library at least twice a week. I harboured a grudge against the English teacher, however, after he belted me for making more than twenty punctuation mistakes in a long passage of Shakespeare which I had learned by heart, and could reproduce word perfect. For colons I had put semicolons, for commas, full stops, and I had omitted several exclamation marks. With a half mark minused for each error, I failed to get the necessary five out of ten to avoid being belted. But I eventually got my own back, in a way which involved no harm except a bruised ego and loss of dignity for the teacher. Revenge was sweet.

The French teacher kept a half bottle of whisky in his desk

drawer, and when trying to teach us became too much, he would hide behind his opened desk lid, unscrew the bottle and take a few glugs.

Then there was the teacher who suddenly, mid-term, disappeared. In the absence of any official explanation as to why he had gone, a story emerged that when punishing miscreants in his room after school, he had not only belted boys on the backside, but had made them do the same to him.

Best of all was the Chemistry teacher. Some teachers could control the class with the raising of an eyebrow, but Mr Husband, who we called Hubby to his face, had no control over his class whatsoever. How I looked forward to his lessons! He was a short, overweight, balding man and we were a merciless class, making sure no experiment ever worked. We ran around lighting all the gas jets that came out of the top of the lab desks. We mixed around the labels of his chemical jars. We played endless games of shove halfpenny down the length of the long laboratory desks, and of course we hid his belt, not that anyone would have stood still long enough to receive it. On one rare occasion when we were quietly writing down information we needed for an exam, Hubby was slowly pacing behind us as we perched on high lab stools. As he passed me he whipped out a red rubber gas pipe he had concealed up his sleeve and wrapped it around my bare legs as hard as he could. It really hurt. 'Hubby, what's that for?' I shouted. 'I'm doing nothing wrong.'

'You were cheeky to me a couple of weeks ago, sonny,' he answered, and went to unlock the cupboard where he kept a notebook full of names of the boys from whom he had to exact retribution, and scored mine off.

Almost every lesson would end with him chasing someone around the lab, red-faced and out of breath, with the onlookers goading him on. He was easily the most popular teacher in the school. Several years after he retired I was walking along a busy

Edinburgh Street when I saw this figure in front of me whose shape and gait were unmistakable. 'Hubby!' I called out. He turned, recognised, and even seemed pleased to see me. He told me over a pint how much he missed those days, despite our atrocious behaviour.

At school, I was no stranger to the belt. Most of the staff had their own preferred model – some with several thongs, others with just two. There were favoured techniques as well, some inflicting the punishment on both hands others just on one. Some made you roll your sleeves up, trying to make the belt hit hard on the softer skin of the lower arm. Some would whip the belt up after the downstroke to try and catch you on the underside of the arm, but if you were quick and knew this was coming, you could move your hands away. If you were lucky, the teacher would hit himself, much to the joy of the watching class.

This violence was perpetuated by the prefects, who, without any reference to a higher authority, could physically punish any pupil they felt like with a gym shoe. Bullying was rife, but I was more fortunate than many by having a big brother at school who I could always rely on to come to my rescue if necessary.

School could be a scary place sometimes, but so could home. Our father had no qualms about taking a stick to Robin or me if we misbehaved. Indeed, if he found out we had been belted by a teacher, he would often add another beating for misbehaving at school. Talk about a double whammy!

'Spare the rod and spoil the child' might have been in his parental instruction book. Many of my school friends also came from families where they would be physically beaten by their fathers, in some cases not just for misdemeanours but for failing to do well in class.

I don't think Tony was intentionally cruel and at the time it was culturally acceptable for a parent to chastise a child. 'This will hurt me more than it will hurt you,' was the cliché he would churn out before laying into me with a stick. In future years, when a practising social worker, I would have had no choice but to remove a child being similarly treated from his family, for their own safety, and the parent would face the full sanction of the law. But the punishment for my father was that his behaviour effectively destroyed our relationship. He became a man to fear, not love; someone to mistrust, and in later years to avoid. It was not until I was much older and wiser that I realised it was himself he was punishing. His anger was displaced and I was the unfortunate scapegoat for his own unresolved issues.

Equally difficult to understand and come to terms with was his lack of interest in his children. A skilled fisherman and musician, he loved the outdoors and had many practical abilities, yet never spent time sharing these with his family. He had folders full of press cuttings singing his praises as an accomplished rugby player and promised to attend every game if I made it into the school first fifteen. I never missed a match. He missed them all. Years later, when I told him how disappointed I had been by this, he threw me out of the house. It was midnight, in Glencoe, in winter. That was the evening I learned the meaning of friendship though, when after phoning my Edinburgh flatmates they drove into the night to bring me home.

The school had a compulsory cadet force and every Friday when lessons were over we paraded in army uniform on the tarmac in front of the school building whilst the janitor hurled verbal abuse at us. He was an ex-company sergeant major, typical of his kind, powerfully built and with a voice like a foghorn. Every summer we had a week's cadet camp, as often as not held in old army barracks at Cultybraggan, just outside Comrie, some eight miles from Crieff. Here we would rush about on the hills, carrying .303 rifles, having mild explosives called thunder-flashes thrown at our feet, battling over assault courses, firing at images of German soldiers and being taught where to aim a rifle if we wanted to kill someone. Inevitably, alcohol was smuggled in, and the ensuing underage drinking would end with fights breaking out in the hut. One evening I got into an argument with fellow pupil and erstwhile friend George, a local Crieff lad. The two of us reported to the sick bay the next morning, George with a black eye and I with a swollen hand. We made up some implausible excuse as to what had happened. Our punishment was to be deprived of running around the hills above Comrie being shouted at, and instead spending the day confined to the barracks, 'guarding' 'the huts. What a result! But it was to get better. The brigadier responsible for school cadet forces in Scotland made an unannounced visit, and was no doubt disappointed to find no-one there other than George and myself. We, however, said all the right things, showed him around and spoke enthusiastically about the joys of the CCF, which we both hated.

'Well, boys, what do you want to do when you leave school?' he asked.

'Join the Army, sir,' we both lied in unison. He took our names, thanked us, and left.

Some months later, the brigadier wrote to Captain Bell, the physics teacher who was the senior officer in charge of the school cadet force, describing his visit to Cultybraggan, including the conversation he had had with George and myself. So impressed he was by our desire to join the Army he had made arrangements for us to travel to Edinburgh where we would be put up in a hotel, and spend a week as observers and guests of the Army, in Sandhurst, the national officer training academy. We were to be wined and dined and treated as VIP guests. And this was to happen in term-time! There were boys in the school who would have given their eye-teeth for this opportunity, but for it to go to two of the most unlikely pupils interested in that way of life was, for us, sublime. I was fifteen, and it was my first trip south of the border.

Tony, meanwhile, had started a new career. He had been dabbling in antiques, scouring junk shops and auctions for things he could sell at a profit, and although he had a good eye for what might make money, he needed to do something different.

'I am interested in teaching History,' he told Mr Maine, the headmaster of Ardvreck Preparatory School in Crieff. The school provided an education up until what was then called the common entrance exam, the gateway for well-heeled boys to even more expensive and exclusive schools.

'Grand, when can you start?' was the reply, and within a few days Tony, with no qualifications, experience or training, was confronting a class of pupils whose parents were paying considerable sums to have their boys educated. It turned out, by all accounts, that he was a dedicated and gifted teacher, and with the bonus of his rugby experience, he became a useful addition to the school staff. The pay, however, was poor, and to make ends meet Tony had to find a way of utilising the long school holidays lucratively. He thus embarked upon yet another income-generating scheme.

'That semi-ruined cottage over there, I am told it belongs to you?' he asked a surprised elderly man who had answered the door to his knocking. 'I'll give you fifty pounds for it.' He was standing outside a farmer's house on the island of Lismore.

After some debate, a price was agreed. This happened twice on Lismore, and many of our subsequent holidays were spent in one or other of these cottages as Tony set about their restoration. Again he had no experience, but he was quick to ask for advice and soon learned from his mistakes. The holidays for the rest of us, however, were pretty miserable. We squeezed into a caravan until the cottage was watertight, then camped inside with no running water or electricity. Even in summer it was damp and cold. Tony had little time for us, spending his days on the restoration, and when he did take an occasional day off, it was to go fishing. Robin and I were left to spend our days exploring the island as best we could. We started playing on a large mound of earth about half a mile away from one of the cottages. There, we uncovered human remains, which turned out to be prehistoric. We had discovered a Bronze Age burial site! The site was duly reported, but remains one of the many unexcavated ancient sites on Lismore.

The cottages were eventually rented out as holiday homes, providing a source of much needed income. Next up was very different and proved to be an important venue for the family for many years. On a whim, Ursula had taken her father for a walk around the island of Kerrera, and was immediately captivated by its wild beauty. She persuaded Tony to repeat the walk with her and he too was smitten. They approached Madam MacDougall, Clan Chief and owner of the island.

'We have fallen in love with Kerrera!' they exclaimed, standing on the doorstep of her house just outside Oban.

'I am not surprised, you had better come in,' was the reply. When they left some hours later, it was with instructions to go to visit the estate factor and, with her blessing, to be allowed to rent an empty property. Thus 'Gylen Park' came under family control and remained so for the next fifty years. Built originally as a farmhouse, it was in a superb location at the southern tip of the island, commanding views to Scarba, Luing, the Garvellachs, Mull, and on a clear day, Colonsay and Jura. It had been lying empty for some time, and was in need of substantial repairs but nothing outwith Tony's self-taught skills. A tank was installed to catch the water from a spring on the hill and the house was then plumbed for running water. Missing slates were replaced, walls were repaired and eventually decorated. Although often resistant to leaving Crieff and despite the three-mile walk from the ferry, we children loved it there. The shoreline was dramatic, with the ruins of Gylen Castle standing proud on a nearby promontory. It was as though we had a huge playground to ourselves, full of discoveries, where our imaginations could run riot. We would disappear from dawn to dusk, beachcombing, going out to the salmon nets with Hamish, the local farmer, sea fishing off the rocks, finding caves, building rafts, and of course never coming home empty-handed, as the fire in the hearth that night depended on what driftwood we could find on the shore. We went there at every opportunity, summer and winter. There was no electricity and the long winter nights were spent listening to the erratic reception of a battery-powered radio by the light of a hissing brass tilley lamp, which periodically needed pumping up before the light failed completely.

Eventually mains electricity came to the island and Tony bought a book on how to wire a house. He followed the instructions, and the book did the rounds of the other houses on the island as each occupier took it upon themselves to wire their own property. All but the schoolhouse were wired in this way, as being Council-owned it merited the skills of professional electricians. Before the electricity board would flick the switch connecting the island to mains supply, each building had to be inspected. The schoolhouse was the only one that failed.

Back in Crieff, we moved to my grandparent's house in Burrell Street. My grandmother was an austere, and to me as a child, frightening woman, always dressed in black, never smiling, and constantly complaining. After she died, she was always the example my father used whenever I expressed any negativity.

'She was negative, and what happened to her?' he would shout at me.

'She died,' he would make me reply, as though expressing anything seen to be critical or pessimistic would immediately see me somehow struck down. I did not have the courage to point out that she was an old lady who lived well beyond her life expectancy. Following her death, my grandfather moved to Gigha, where Jo, Robin and I had some happy holidays, enjoying his kindness and generosity. These were our first holidays away from our own parents.

We moved into his Crieff house – a three-storey terraced house on a busy street, about a fifteen-minute walk away from school. Money was still very tight and life was somewhat spartan. The family car was an old second-hand post office van which we all piled into for the journeys to Oban to catch the Kerrera or Lismore ferries, journeys which were constantly delayed by one other of us children, usually me, being car sick. The only heating allowed in the house was in the kitchen where the coke fire which heated the water was never off in the winter, and it was this that we huddled around trying to keep warm. There was no central heating, and on rare occasions a single-bar electric fire was switched on in the sitting room. For much of the winter the window in the bedroom I shared with my brother in the attic would be covered with intricate patterns of frost on the inside. I rigged up a string-pull system which allowed me to switch off the light by the door at the other end of the room without having to get out of bed into the sub-zero temperatures.

Tony worked all the hours he could, spending what spare time he had photocopying his collection of ancient maps, colouring around the coast, and framing them for sale. A sign on the window on Burrell Street was for the sale of the honey he collected from his eighteen bee-hives. Ursula also was industrious, providing three meals a day for two growing boys and her husband, on a very limited budget, as well as doing all the household duties without any outside help. We never ate out, convenience food was a thing of the future, and there were no family luxuries or treats. I would get the occasional odd job from neighbours and saved every penny until I could buy a second-hand bike for a pound from an Italian called Guido who had a junk shop nearby. It was lethal, but worked. To brake, you had to back-pedal, and naturally there were no gears, but this liberated me to go off on Sundays on long cycling trips. It was a new-found freedom which I cherished.

When Robin left school to go to Edinburgh University, Tony got a teaching job in Ayrshire, and I was boarded out for a couple of years. Sometimes this was privately with a family, but mostly it was in Ogilvie House, one of the official school boarding houses.

Ever entrepreneurial, Tony set about another project which again was to have profound implications for all the family. In 1965 he bought an old caravan, cut a hole in the side to create a counter, had some signs professionally made and started selling teas, coffees and hamburgers from a lay-by on the Black Mount, on the approach road to Glencoe. 'The Pie Van', as we called it, provided more income in the summer months than his annual teaching salary. Initially we lived in a caravan he had moved from a Lismore rebuild, but Tony had seen a derelict cottage in Glencoe and was able to purchase this for a negligible outlay. Again we were spending holidays and many weekends camping in a damp cottage, which became marginally more bearable after mains electricity and water were connected. I would cycle there from Crieff on my ancient bike just to have the freedom of mobility whilst in Glencoe.

Whilst at this cottage, Tony set his sights on a old roofless byre nearby. It was detached from the house that formed part of the same property. The house had been empty for a number of years and was uninhabitable, but what caught Tony's eye was the location. The buildings were right alongside the busy A82, the arterial road to the West Highlands of Scotland. And they were for sale. He had just sold one of the Lismore cottages and the other was quickly put on the market. Money was raised and the ruins bought. Tony retired from teaching, moved into another caravan in the garden of the new property and worked there, mostly alone, on its restoration. When it was finished, it became an outlet for his passion for antiques.

Meanwhile, I was fast approaching my last year at school. With Tony occupied on rebuilding the ruined property in Glencoe, Ursula stayed behind in Crieff to look after me. Robin was at university and Jo was moving to Africa. She had met and married Alan Grey, a tall, gentle man, who instantly fitted in well with the rest of the family. Alan had graduated from Newcastle University with a degree in Animal Husbandry and was keen to put his agricultural knowledge and skills to good use. Jo had not been given the opportunity to go to university, something she made up for in later life, and had trained as a nursery nurse. She had worked with children in Wales and London before meeting Alan. Their wedding in the ancient Lismore Church was blessed with sunshine and goodwill. They made a striking couple, Jo in white, with her long blonde hair tied up on her head and always with a happy smile, Alan in his kilt, quietly directing operations, making sure everyone was OK. Robin had been spending the summer in America, and his appearance had changed, causing some parental consternation. I was envious of his newfound freedom, and like Jo, I was delighted to see him. After the reception in the island hall, they were taken off in Alan's brother John's old wooden trawler. The rest of us drove up to the north end of the island to wave as they sailed past. John, not untypically, came in a bit too close, and hit the sandbank. The boat juddered to a halt, and there, with a falling tide, it stayed, refusing to budge for the next twelve hours. Fortunately, Jo and Alan did not have to spend their wedding night in a bunk listing at forty-five degrees, but were taken off to a local hotel.

Alan had got a prestigious job as an agricultural development officer in rural Zambia, and some months after the wedding they started their new life there. Soon, Jo had babies of her own to look after. As the summer holidays of 1967 approached I was keen to do something on my own. Anything which did not involve living in a cold caravan and working every day in the pie van was attractive. I was developing a sense of spiritual curiosity, beginning to appreciate perhaps that there was something undefinable missing from my life, like a gnawing hunger that goes away after a meal but returns. It was something I could not ignore. When I was told about a week-long summer camp in West Linton, outside Edinburgh, run by the Scripture Union, I signed up.

The camp was very much what one might expect. A bunch of kids drawn from schools across Scotland, spending the day running around, playing games, making a lot of noise and generally having fun. After dinner in the evening the Christian element kicked in and the trainee ministers who were running the show broke us up into small discussion groups where Christian theology was expounded. It all seemed fine to me. The strength and depth of the faith of the leaders was impressive.

On the last night I stayed behind and asked the group leader, 'OK I am convinced. What do you have to do to become a Christian, to lead a Christian life?'

'You accept Jesus as your saviour, you say your prayers, and go to Church,' was the reply.

The disappointment I felt was profound. I did all of these things, but there was something missing, something so essential, that if this was all that was on offer it was not for me. It felt like a teaching which had no heart and offered no prospect of personal development or spiritual growth. It seemed a cold theology, although full of wonderful stories. For me, it contained no real spiritual path, no way of contacting the unboundedness of being I felt sure existed, no sense of a journey for the soul. I began to look elsewhere.

That proved challenging. The school library contained nothing on alternative religion or eastern philosophy. The town library was more promising and there I discovered T. Lobsang Rampa whose book *The Third Eye* was purportedly about the life of a Tibetan monk, whose weird experiences enthralled me. The stories he told of the occult, paranormal, mystical life he had led I found irresistible and I soaked it up, getting hold of as many of his books as the library would order up for me. Eventually, however, I began to find them repetitive, spotting inconsistencies in his storytelling. Years later I discovered that he was in fact a plumber from Devon and had never been to Tibet in his life. But his books, despite being based on a lie, had kindled a flame of fascination for Eastern thought which I have never lost.

I found the plethora of Hindu deities confusing. I tried to learn about the difference schools of Buddhism, but struggled with the finer issues. But I read and re-read anything I could lay my hands on about all of the various Eastern belief systems. And it just became more and more fascinating. I read biographies, autobiographies, the Upanishads, the Mahabharata, the Bhagavad Gita, Lao Tzu. I wrote to a London publisher of Eastern literature and was sent more and more to feed my insatiable curiosity. The common theme emerging was that through meditation it was possible to achieve a state of spiritual liberation or enlightenment, and that you needed a master or guru to help you along the path.

It is said that the right teacher appears at the right time. Tony and Ursula used to buy the *Sunday Observer*, and I would flick through the magazine section they left lying around. One issue contained an article about an Indian who had just come out of the Himalayas and was teaching something called Transcendental Meditation. There was a photo of him in a white silk dhoti and sporting long black hair and beard. He was on a mission to spiritually regenerate the West with this technique of meditation, which he claimed was simple but very effective. There was a contact address in London, to which I wrote to find out more. I was told that I would need to be taught this meditation technique by someone who had been trained personally by the guru, Maharishi Mahesh Yogi, and she gave me an address in Edinburgh where I needed to go for the four days it took to learn the technique. I knew that this was what I wanted to do but was frustrated in that it was going to be impossible to achieve whilst I was still at school and living in Crieff. My plans to learn TM went on hold.

I decided I would just have to create techniques for myself. Late at night, I would sit cross-legged on my bed staring at candles, or trying to still my thoughts, watching my breathing, and anything else I could think of or utilise from my extensive reading. Mostly I got bored, lay down and went to sleep, but sometimes the experiences were extraordinary and very powerful, and convinced me that I was on to something important. One in particular occurred several times over the year I was doing this, something which took two forms but had the same end result. Sitting there in stillness and silence, I would feel myself, my whole sense of physical and mental being, getting bigger and bigger, expanding slowly, my awareness filling first the room I was in, then the house, the street, the town; my boundaries expanding and expanding until, almost with a pop, there were no boundaries left and I just was, but with no sense of me, just this all-encompassing awareness. The alternative experience had the same end result, where I would feel my being getting smaller and smaller, until it would disappear altogether and all I was left with was the wonderful sense of totality, of an all-encompassing being with no sense of individuality. These were awakening experiences, the residues of which have stayed with me since, and provided a foundation of understanding which has guided my life.

Naturally I would talk to my friends about Maharishi and meditation, but no-one I knew was interested. A passing fad, they no doubt thought; he will get over it. And then, out of the blue, every schoolboy's heroes, The Beatles, were sitting at Maharishi's feet, extolling the virtues of practising TM. I felt so vindicated! This man I had been talking about endlessly was now a household name and constantly in the news. But my elevated status was short-lived; it was time to leave school.

The principle exams of the day, 'Highers', were sat at the beginning of the summer term. I had studied hard for them, sitting night after night in the freezing kitchen trying to get to grips with calculus and trigonometry, my attention focused more on Radio Luxembourg or Radio Caroline, the offshore stations playing the kind of music to which I wanted to listen. The remainder of the term when the exams were over was spent doing nothing particularly creative.

'I would like to leave school at half term,' I pleaded to Mr Quick. A tall, thin man with greasy, swept-back grey hair, he had been the headmaster throughout my school career, and was a significant authority figure in my life. His rule was law, and woe betide anyone who crossed him.

'Boys from Morrison's Academy do not leave school early,' was the stern reply.

I had got myself an evening job in the cocktail bar of a local hotel, the Murray Park, at the top end of Crieff. It was legal, I was of an age to serve alcohol, and it was a useful source of income. I was there less than a week when Mr Quick walked in with his wife, took one look at me serving behind the bar and walked out again. It was beneath his dignity to be served by one of his pupils. I was called up the next day at school and summoned to his office. The last time I had been there I had been belted. It was a room with unpleasant memories.

'Cooper,' he started, 'I recall you asking if you could leave school at half term. Well under the circumstances I think this could be arranged.' He was clearly looking forward to seeing the back of me, but having made this decision for one, he had to allow the others who wanted to leave early to go as well.

As a result, some ten days later there were about twenty early leavers called into the school library. The headmaster told us how sad he would be to see us go, but that we would always have the benefits of the old boys' club, a world-wide network of ex-Morrisonians who would be there to help us. We were told to come back the following morning, bringing money for the old boys school tie which he would formally present us with.

After morning assembly we duly filed into the library. Mr Quick entered a few minutes later walking fast and tall, his long black cloak swishing about in his slipstream. He told us again about what a wonderful organisation we were about to sign up for, The Morrison's Academy for Boys ex-pupils club.

I was first on his list. 'Cooper' he called, old boys' tie in one hand, the other extended to take my money.

'I am not joining, sir,' I said. He wasn't sure if he heard me correctly and asked me to repeat myself.

'I am not joining the old boys' club,' I said, calmly and slowly, although inside I was quaking with fear. 'I want to stand on my own two feet, sir, and not be dependent on favours handed down to me because I have had a privileged education. Thank you, sir, but no thank you.'

To this day, I have never seen anyone so angry. He turned purple with rage, and for a moment I thought he was going to take a swing at me. But he managed to control himself enough to shout, 'You have taken the best the school has to offer, years of dedicated teaching have brought you to this, where you are about to go to university. You owe the school everything, and now you are turning round and kicking it and us in the face.'

To be on the receiving end of such anger was scary, but I

CHAPTER THREE

Istanbul and the Summer of Love

Half the blasted idiots are stuck in Yugoslavia
With hardly a Dina
And looking no cleaner
'Nobody's Got Any Money in the Summer'—Roy Harper

'Where are you going, son?' the driver asked as he gently brought his lorry to a halt beside me. It was a few minutes after five a.m., raining, the yellow light from the street lamps shimmering in the puddles. Dawn was struggling to make an impression on the night sky. I had left home and was heading south towards the edge of town, thumb out, not expecting anyone to stop so soon. This was the first vehicle that had come by me.

'Istanbul,' I replied with a smile as I heaved my rucksack and body onto the passenger seat.

'I cannae take you there, son,' he said, 'but I can take you as far as Manchester. How's that?'

'Just grand,' I said. I had only recently turned eighteen. My physical, emotional and spiritual journeying had begun.

In 1968, the UK economy was in dire straits. In order to prevent money from leaving the country, Harold Wilson's Labour Government had placed a limit of fifty pounds on the amount of cash anyone was allowed to take abroad. This was before the days of credit cards or travellers cheques, and this fifty pound limit rule was rigidly enforced. Having had an acceptance from Edinburgh University I was eligible to use their student travel service, and had obtained a cheap one-way flight to Ljubljana, in Yugoslavia. I was not quite sure where it was, but it did get me out of the more expensive parts of Europe where fifty pounds would have quickly disappeared. I had told my parents I was going grape picking, but my dream was to head further East. I had read that a bunch of the original Haight Ashbury hippies from San Francisco had moved to a rooftop in Istanbul, and like a moth to a flame I felt irresistibly drawn.

Darkness had once more descended and it was still raining when my last lift dropped me off outside a tube station in London. I knew nobody in the city, had no family there, no friends or contacts. I had booked myself into a youth hostel in Earls Court for a couple of nights, thinking I would give myself a day to see some of the more famous sights before catching the flight. I wandered out that evening feeling somewhat overwhelmed, my first time in such a big city. I headed for King's Road in Chelsea as I had been told it was the hippest part of town, and found myself, pint in hand, propping up the bar in a pub called The Six Bells.

I could barely believe my eyes. The place was buzzing with the most extraordinary looking people. I tried to look cool and fit in, but the reality is that I must have stood out like a sore thumb. My hair was still short, as I was only just out of school, and my conventional clothes, jeans and a t-shirt, looked drab in comparison to the blaze of colours others were wearing. The bar was filled with the most beautiful women I had ever seen, many with long blonde hair, some wearing loose, brightly-coloured skirts, others with hot pants so short that they may as well have not bothered. There were semi-transparent tops, beads and bangles, colourful headscarves, strappy sandals, and all were having a wonderful time, smiling, chatting and laughing, some in big groups, others wrapped around their boyfriends.

The guys seemed to be the epitome of cool, with their beards, shoulder-length hair, velvet bell-bottom trousers, brightly coloured shirts, beads and little round shades. They used a vocabulary that was unfamiliar to me: 'cool man' and 'far out' were not words used in Crieff. One fellow, who looked impossibly thin, leaned over the bar beside me and with a strong Glaswegian accent ordered some drinks.

'From Scotland?' I asked, feeling stupid. It was obvious where he was from.

'Aye,' he said. 'And you?'

'Just arrived, hitched down from Crieff this morning.'

'Wow, that's cool. On your own? I'm in with a group of pals, come and join us if you want.'

I needed no second invitation. He introduced himself as Jim, he was with his brother Ronnie, and a small group of guys who looked to be in their mid-twenties, and who were clearly well-known in the pub. They had a few questions to ask of me, and I found out later that they were a little suspicious of strangers in their midst as the London drug squad was reputedly trying to infiltrate the hippie culture; my youth and naivety soon allayed any suspicions. Despite living in Wimbledon, The Six Bells was their regular haunt. We had a couple of pints and arranged to meet again the following evening.

I spent the next day sight-seeing and by early evening was back in The Six Bells. Jim and Ronnie were there, and with them a Mancunian called Charlie, in his early twenties, currently unemployed, and living with the brothers in Wimbledon. He was a little taciturn at first, but became chattier as the pints came in. With shoulder-length hair and bushy sideburns, he lived for blues music and was an expert on the subject, waxing lyrical about the fretboard skills of artists I had never heard of.

Jim and Ronnie had also come from a provincial background in the West of Scotland, and had moved to London to find work. Jim was the older and more serious of the two, but both were empathetic to my situation, having just arrived in the city, and said I was welcome to stay in their flat when I returned from my travels.

The following afternoon I landed in Ljubljana in Yugoslavia, my first taste of a foreign country. All my senses were on full alert. I had never felt the sun so hot on my face before. The smells of the street were different, the sounds strange. It felt alien, but not threatening. I latched onto a small group of Irish students and headed for the university, where cheap accommodation was available, and ended up in a dormitory with five other occupants. One in particular intrigued me. Older than the others in the room, he had packed in university in his third year, and headed off, overland, to India. He had had all kinds of adventures and misadventures, falling ill, being robbed, losing his passport and eventually running out of money, and was now on his way home. The only possession he had with him was a sitar bought in Rishikesh that had travelled with him carefully wrapped up in his sleeping bag. A colourful character in every sense, and full of travellers' tales, I told him I was heading out to Istanbul. He gave me a couple of suggestions of rooftops to sleep on and where to find them, and said the dope there was plentiful and very cheap, if that was what I was after. We joined up with the Irish girls and went to a bar where the locals encouraged us to sample the local brew, slivovitz, a strong, plum-based brandy which burned the back of the throat and left me with a headache.

Ljubljana is not a big place and it did not take me long to get to the edge of town and start hitch-hiking on the main road east. I had a small map of Europe in my back pocket, on which I had highlighted a route, which effectively was as straight a line as possible connecting the main cities between me and Turkey.

Sometimes I slept rough, bedding my sleeping bag down in a field or empty barn, which was fine if a little chilly first thing in the morning. Occasionally a driver would allow me to sleep in the back of his truck, and once I was taken in by an elderly farmer and his wife, fed, and given the spare room. People were always kind and helpful. Communication was a constant struggle, not having a word of the language, but I muddled through.

By the time I reached Belgrade I had seen nothing of the country, which made me want to stop and explore more. The capital itself was disappointing. I gave myself a couple of days' break from the road, but was glad to move on. It felt like I was being pulled by a magnet, further and further east. I knew where I wanted to get to, and was impatient to arrive.

The Yugoslav countryside was changing, but still uninspiring. Mile after endless mile of straight, cobbled surface, with alternating sections of massive concrete paving. There were no lanes. The road was just about wide enough for two vehicles to pass if one was prepared to put two wheels off the prepared surface onto the dirt, and meeting every oncoming vehicle precipitated a game of chicken to see who would give way first. Lorries always won this against other smaller vehicles, but it would get quite scary when two lorries met. Bumpy, dusty and dry, I soon tired of days on straight, boring roads bordered by endless fields of melon crops or corn, with the farmers' wives at roadside stalls holding high their produce in a vain attempt to persuade people to stop and buy. Lifts from farmers were short and slow. Lifts on lorries were better but scarier, especially when the driver was either struggling to stay awake, or putting a brick on the accelerator to rest his foot. I have never subsequently been on a road where there were so many crashes. Upturned lorries, burnt-out cars and rusting chassis littered the route all the way to the border and beyond. When I was leaving a town called Niš, a car slowed down for me, but it was already quite full, no space for me and my backpack, so I waved it on. When I got a lift an hour later we soon hit a massive traffic jam, the cause of which turned out to be a crash involving the same car that I so nearly took a ride in. Judging by the wreckage, anyone inside would have been lucky to survive.

The border crossing into Bulgaria was smooth and I found myself in a country which was hotter, poorer and cheaper, with a peasant population grinding a basic living from the land. Most of the passing vehicles were horse-drawn carts, and tourist cars were a rarity. Hence, soon after leaving Sofia I was surprised to see a new-looking Mercedes approaching and even more surprised when it stopped for me. My surprise turned to delight when the German couple said they were going to Istanbul.

In their early thirties and on holiday, they had driven from Munich, and, I suspect, were getting fed up with each other's company, cooped up in the car together day after day, and had picked me up to relieve their boredom. Their English was fluent and I enjoyed speaking again after many days of enforced silence. When we stopped for food they insisted I ate with them as their guest. When we stopped for the night they looked for the best accommodation they could find, leaving me to find my own.

For the next three days we kept driving east. The state of the roads made for slow progress. He was an impatient driver and would shout at local peasants to move faster out of his way, orders which were an embarrassment to hear and were largely ignored. Generous to a fault, he could be loud and aggressive. His wife was softer and gentler, and I could see she found him exasperating on occasion.

There was a long queue of vehicles at the Turkish border and it took us several hours to get through. We stopped as the day was dimming at Edirne, arriving in time to see the sun setting behind the magnificent mosque, with the local muezzin on the minaret calling the faithful to prayer. It was the first time I had heard the sound and was mesmerised. It sounded so mysterious, almost mystical. I found accommodation in a local hostel, and was shown around the mosque by a group of local students who were very curious to meet a traveller from the West.

By mid-afternoon the following day I was dropped off in the old part of Istanbul. The next three months were to be life-changing.

Within an hour I was sitting in a room of the Gülhane Park Hotel smoking my first joint. I had found the place easily from directions I had been given, down a sidestreet near the Hagia Sophia mosque. A flickering neon sign was all that identified the building on the outside. Inside, there was a narrow, twisting stair allowing access to the four storeys and the roof. Initially I opted for a bed in a room, and handed in my passport to a seedy-looking character at the front desk. I wondered if I would ever see it again.

The room had crumbling wallpaper, cracked plaster and large patches of damp on the ceiling. I found an empty bed, threw my backpack on it, sat down and looked around. There were about eight people in the room and they seemed welcoming. Unlike the smart, trendy hippies of Earls Court, these were, like me, in jeans or shorts, and t-shirts. All had at least shoulder-length hair, or a massive frizz ball of curls. The room was mixed sex and nationalities, some Dutch, some Americans, and a couple of very attractive Swedish girls chatting to each other in the corner of the room. I was the only one from the UK. One of the Dutchmen was rolling a joint, which he lit up and passed across to me.

I was glad no-one was paying much attention. The cannabis was rolled in tobacco, and I had never smoked anything before, so dealing with the effects of both and trying to remain cool about the process was impossible. I coughed and spluttered, and quickly passed the joint on. I had just about recovered when it came my way again. More coughing, more spluttering. The Dutchman appreciated my predicament.

'Just breathe it in and hold your breath,' he said, 'you'll be fine.' I lay on my bed internally searching for symptoms of being stoned. I felt relaxed, and was aware of the damp patches on the ceiling forming pictures in my mind. It was unnerving to see that one formed a profile of my father's face. I became a little withdrawn and drifted off to sleep.

Staying in a room with a bed was more expensive than living on the rooftop, which had a charge equivalent to twenty-five pence a night. Having so little money I soon moved up and found a corner to myself. This was to be home for the next ten weeks. The Swedish girls had moved up with me, and occupied the same corner as myself. I lusted after one of them, whose lithe figure, long black hair, sparkling eyes and even more sparkling personality, made her irresistible. Ulrika was twenty-five, seven years older than me, and although she befriended me, did not see me as a potential lover. In any case, privacy on the rooftop was non-existent, but she laid her sleeping bag next to mine and sometimes in the early hours of a cold morning I would find her cuddled up beside me. The girls were fun, lively and popular, and being associated with them meant that in no time I was fully assimilated into life on the rooftop.

The days soon slipped into some kind of a pattern. The rooftop had no protection from the sun and it was hard to sleep beyond daybreak. Someone would go out and buy bread and cheese from a street vendor, and this would be shared, as would the first joint of the day, which would make its way around the rooftop. The local Turkish cannabis was in plentiful supply and very cheap, the main supplier being an American from San Francisco who had been living on the roof for the last six months, long enough for him to find his own sources.

Most of us would hang about on the roof in the morning, swapping stories and dreaming about the future. Many were heading to India, some were on their way back. Most had come from middle-class backgrounds which they had rejected to drop out and turn on. All had dreams about a better way to lead a life, and many hours were spent formulating ideas about a perfect social and political order. I was different from most in that I had decided that I wanted to go to university.

'Don't bother with that bourgeois crap, man,' I would be told. 'Free yourself up, come with us to India,' was a much repeated offer.

I would explore the old part of the city in the afternoons, sometimes with others but often alone. I spent many hours sitting in the Blue Mosque absorbing the atmosphere, watching the faithful come and go and marvelling at the beauty of the building. One huge dome dominates the skyline, along with eight smaller ones and six minarets, two hundred stained glass windows, twenty thousand blue tiles and exquisitely carved marble. It was a peaceful place to hang out in, sitting on intricately patterned carpets which covered the entire floor, feeling very mellow and laid-back after a joint in The Pudding Shop.

The Pudding Shop, just across the street from the park where the Blue Mosque stood, was a landmark on the hippie trail. A hunger for something sweet to eat is a common side effect from smoking dope, and the café owners had soon realised this when their clientele, the hippies from the Istanbul rooftops, descended on the place and ignored everything on the menu except puddings. They further catered to the clientele by playing the latest and best of quality music available at the time – The Doors, Jefferson Airplane, Bob Dylan, The Grateful Dead – as well as some wonderful American bluesmen. It was a meeting place, a place to leave messages for people coming after you, a place where you could happily while away an afternoon or an evening, listening to good music in great company and eating... puddings. Puddings of all descriptions; lemon meringue pies, apple pies, cakes filled with cannabis, chocolate cakes, crumbles, the variety was huge, the portions enormous and the cost negligible.

I loved the smells, the noise, and the colours of the city. The setting sun would silhouette the mosque against a sky changing from bright orange to fiery red in a matter of moments. As the red turned to black, the shapes of the domes would become harder to make out, but from the minarets towering above like rockets waiting to launch, the call to prayer of the muezzin would reverberate across the city. On the street directly below, the hot chestnut vendor would be stoking his fire, heating the chestnut-filled pan, calling out for custom, the smell of their cooking, so evocative of winter, drifting up to the rooftop.

Up by the university there was a smaller mosque, less popular with the tourists, but a building I came to love. And adjacent to the rooftop was the Hagia Sophia, another fabulous architectural masterpiece. Its history mirrored that of the city. Originally built as a church, it became a mosque, a Roman Catholic Cathedral, a Greek Orthodox Cathedral and finally a museum. A stone's throw away was the Grand Bazaar and Spice Market often crowded with tourists but useful places to escape the heat of the midday sun.

The rooftop sometimes attracted the attention of the police, but they were seen coming and there was time to extinguish joints before they reached the roof. Anyway, they had come mostly out of boredom and for the opportunity to chat with young western women. Their very occasional presence never disturbed the peaceful atmosphere of the place.

One night, a local radio station was playing softly in the background.

'Quiet, guys,' said one of the girls, 'that's Dylan.' For the next forty minutes we listened transfixed as *John Wesley Harding*, was played in its entirety. It felt like it was being played just for us. The evenings were my favourite time, chatting, smoking dope, listening to music, watching the sun go down behind the minarets and every few hours the muezzin calling the faithful to prayer. These were magical days.

Time passed slowly and lazily. A few of us decided to take a break from the city and jumped on a train to a town further down the coast, but we missed the rooftop and soon returned. August became September, and I had university to go to. It was time to head for home, but therein lay a problem. Not only was I broke, but the 'hotel' manager still had my passport, and I would not get it back unless I paid my dues. The twenty-five pence a night had mounted up and I did not have enough money to pay my bill. I was going to have to do a runner, but I needed my passport. Fortunately, there was a group of six also planning to leave at the same time and they were fully paid up. I wandered empty-handed past the desk, in shorts and a t-shirt, clearly going nowhere, and asked the proprietor for my passport as I needed it for identification to collect poste restante mail. 'Give it right back when you come in,' he said as he handed it over.

'Of course,' I lied and wandered into the street, to be joined a few minutes later by the six who had taken my pack out with theirs. Feeling guilty, I started the long journey home.

~

Almost four decades later I happened to be back in Istanbul, and found myself walking down the street past the Gülhane Park Hotel. I could not resist the temptation to look inside. The place was transformed. Still a hotel, it was clean and smart with a wide sweeping staircase and a bright, new reception desk, where a man was busy with paperwork, barely looking up as I came in. I climbed the stairs, floor by floor, until I reached the door leading to the roof. It was not locked. The rooftop, home for those long weeks, was strewn with hotel detritus. Broken beds and chairs were piled high, along with old fridges and rusting cookers. The memories came flooding back and I had a nostalgic few minutes before closing the door behind me and heading back down.

A few minutes later I passed The Pudding Shop, now a tourist attraction filled with photos from the sixties. There was a tour guide outside, a group of young tourists listening intently.

'This was the home of the hippies,' he was saying, 'this is where they all came to hang out and smoke dope.'

I waited until he had finished, then quickly nipped in front of him to speak to his audience.

'He is quite right, you know, it's all true. And some of us are still here!'

~

I had an uncomfortable night just inside the Bulgarian border where a huge military exercise was taking place. The army was being mobilised following the recent Russian invasion of Czechoslovakia. I tried to rest under a bridge but with tanks crossing over all night sleep was impossible, and I changed my route and headed towards the Greek border. By chance I met up with Ulrika, the Swedish girl from the rooftop, who was also heading home. We got a lift in the back of a farm truck after helping the farmer pick and load red grapes. We slept in his shed, and he dropped us off in the main town the next day.

I was seriously broke, and did not know where the next meal was coming from. I contemplated selling blood in a local hospital, but stories of blood-drained bodies being dragged out of the Bosporus did not make an appealing thought. I got as far as Thessalonica in Northern Greece and used the last of my cash for a night in a local youth hostel. I was still more than a thousand miles from home, and now penniless. There was a notice board in the hostel, and on it a note to say that there was a lift to London leaving from outside the British Embassy in Belgrade at twelve noon in three days' time. I grabbed the note from the board and by six a.m. the following morning I was hitch-hiking again. I hitch-hiked from dawn to dusk. I had been on the edge of a village for hours when a young woman appeared with a tray of hot food. In another town, I was mistaken for a Czech refugee and again given food and shelter. And at ten a.m. on the third morning after leaving Thessalonica I was standing outside the British Embassy in Belgrade.

I asked the receptionist if she knew anything about a lift leaving for London. She said she did not, but that I should check the street outside and look to see who was parked there. As I turned to do that, she asked me for my name as the embassy was commonly used as a poste restante address. There was nothing for me, and I left.

Meanwhile, back in Crieff, Tony and Ursula were beginning to get anxious. I had sent them a postcard from Belgrade on my way out, but selfishly had not communicated since. Neither of them had been prone to worry about me before, and their world was one I was trying to distance myself from. But they were concerned enough to phone the Belgrade Embassy, and later when we compared notes, the conversation they had with an official there took place at the same time I was talking to the receptionist.

'Don't worry, Mr Cooper,' they were told. 'David probably did the same as lots his age group, and went on to Istanbul. He is probably on his way home now.'

Outside, I found the VW camper van, but was disheartened

to read the note on the window. 'Lift offered to London' it said, then underneath 'Sharing petrol costs and driving.' My heart sank. I could do neither of these things. The van owners were a husband and wife called Geoff and Anna, both Londoners. I explained my predicament and said I would be happy to pay my share of the expenses but that it would have to wait until I got back and was working, and that I would also be dependent on them for food during the trip. Thankfully they said that was not a problem and I was welcome to join them. A week later they dropped me off in Earls Court.

'Bring any dope back?' was the first thing Jim asked as he answered my banging on the door of the Wimbledon flat.

'Sorry, no, too risky,' I replied.

That same day I found work as a kitchen porter in a café a short walk from the flat. I was given a sub on my wages and at last had money in my pocket again. I stayed with Ronnie and Jim for three weeks, working most days, heading off to The Six Bells on the weekend evenings. I hooked up with one of my work colleagues, a lively, pretty English student called Liz with spiky brown hair, and she stayed over from time to time in the attic room I was occupying in the flat. Music was important to us all and we had some memorable nights in the Marquee Club in Wardour Street, and at a famous concert in the Roundhouse in Camden where The Doors and Jefferson Airplane performed late into the night.

Autumn was in the air, and it was time to move on. It had been an amazing summer, not just for me personally, but for a whole generation.

'You'd think you lot discovered sex,' my mother would tell me later, and in a way it felt that she was right. The contraceptive pill had provided sexual liberation hitherto unknown. But in practically every other sphere of life, values long held dear were being fundamentally challenged in ways which were positive, creative, and life-affirming. In America, Bob Dylan was almost single-handedly turning the world of popular music on its head. In the UK, The Beatles and the Rolling Stones were doing the same. Politically, socially, spiritually, sexually, musically, artistically, the times really were a'changin, and changing to their core. To be a part of that dream to create the new was a privilege. In the years since 1968 I have never experienced anything close to the creative energy that burst upon us that summer. I was coming of age, and it felt like the world was too.

CHAPTER FOUR

A Misspent Youth?

Edinburgh University in the autumn of 1968 was in recovery from the Muggeridge affair. The University Rector had just resigned over an article on LSD written anonymously by my brother Robin in *Student,* the weekly paper run by and for students. The article had sparked off a furore and there was a witch-hunt for the author and calls for the rustication of the editor. Malcolm Muggeridge was also furious when he was asked to support the campaign for the contraceptive pill to be given freely in the University Health Centre. He was replaced by Kenneth Allsop, a popular BBC political analyst, author and world affairs presenter.

Robin had a one-bedroom flat in Drummond Street, which he rented for a pittance from the university. It was empty, but the block was scheduled for demolition. The university was flattening swathes of the south side of Edinburgh at the time, knocking down Georgian buildings and replacing them with constructions of glass and concrete. It was not uncommon to see Adam fireplaces being broken up or hurled into skips from upper storey windows. This vandalism was halted in the late sixties, but for many streets it was too late. Others, like Drummond Street and its immediate neighbours, survived.

I was desperate to find a place to live and get out of my first digs, where I shared a room with three others and had inflexible meal times with mediocre food. I found a place in Oxford Street, and although it was still sharing a room, it was with only one other and was on a bed-only basis rather than full board. The landlady was Polish, and a delight. My roommate was George Pattison, whose mass of bushy, dark hair and ankle-length leather coat made him stand out in a crowd. From Cambridge, he was studying Psychology. He had piercing eyes and a very sharp intellect. Our conversations were nearly always about the four things important to us at the time – sex, drugs, politics and rock 'n' roll – specifically the wild 'underground' bands which were rapidly becoming more mainstream, and American and British blues. Charlie, the Mancunian I had met in The Six Bells, also came to live there for a while, and we spent a lot of time in The Meadow Bar in Buccleuch Street discussing the relative merits and demerits of musicians, and fantasising about the female students in our respective classes. Back at our digs, George and Charlie would cook a macrobiotic concoction of brown rice and tinned lotus roots, the healthy aspect of which was probably negated by the joint which followed.

The University Blues Society had organised a bus to Newcastle to a concert featuring such musical heroes as B.B. King, Sonny Terry and Brownie McGhee, and Fleetwood Mac. The gig was superb. What we had not realised was that there were, in fact, two separate concerts, back to back with the same bands. We decided to buy tickets for the second show and persuaded the bus driver to stay. But we could not find everyone in the group to get the message across so I volunteered to go backstage to speak to the compere, a blues singer, later to become better known as a ballad singer called Long John Baldry. Venturing through the stage door, I found the musicians and passed the message on.

'Hey, son, d'ya want a drink?'

This was an offer from B.B. King. I sat down in this illustrious company, a little overawed, but soon relaxed into the situation. Fortunately Charlie had taught me a little about American blues musicians, some of them quite obscure, and most of them their friends. I could hear the music from the stage filtering back, but I spent the rest of the evening backstage drinking, laughing and joking with these musical legends.

Finally it was time for B.B. King to get back on stage. His band had preceded him and were starting to play.

'Pass me Lucille, son,' he asked. I had been holding his famous guitar. He stood up, shook my hand and walked out. The tumultuous applause that greeted him when he reached the stage shook the building.

A little earlier Sonny Terry, who was blind, had asked me to show him where the toilets were. He took my arm as I led him in the right direction.

'You don't mind a black man taking your arm, son?' he asked in his southern drawl. I said it was an honour.

'Where the hell have you been?' whispered George as I slid back into my seat to catch the last of B.B. King's set.

'You just wouldn't believe it,' I replied, settling back to enjoy the music.

That was the second trip south by bus that year. The first, this time organised by the Socialist Society, or SocSoc, was to London to the Grosvenor Square anti-Vietnam war demonstration. Ten thousand of us from across the UK turned up for the event, the biggest of its kind to date. One of the left-wing political leaders at the time was a Pakistani radical Tariq Ali, who had been described in parliament as 'foreign scum.'

'We are all foreign scum,' we chanted as we ran down Fleet Street, heading for the American Embassy in Grosvenor Square with the intent of taking the building over. However, there were mounted policemen who had other ideas and the situation turned nasty. Violence broke out, and things became scary for both police and demonstrators. Vanessa Redgrave and Tariq Ali were allowed into the embassy to deliver a petition, and eventually things calmed down. This was just as well. The American Embassy is regarded as American territory where US laws apply; the marines protecting the inside of the building were under orders to shoot any demonstrator unlawfully gaining access.

I was very keen to find my own room in a flat. George was moving into nearby Lutton Place, and Charlie had temporarily left town. One evening, I was in the original Traverse Theatre at James Court, just off the Lawnmarket, explaining my accommodation predicament to Pat Finlay, a Sociology student I had met through SocSoc.

'There's an empty room in the flat I'm in,' she told me. 'Come round and see what you think.'

Sure enough, there was a room available in the basement of this two-storey tenement flat. On the ground-floor there was a very large front room, with a high, corniced ceiling and curtainless windows facing onto Lauriston Place. The room was empty of all furniture and felt quite stark and cold. It was being used as a playroom by the three-year-old daughter of Ingrid and Ian Winbush, aka 'Windy', who had been in the flat for a year but were about to leave for America. Off this room was an empty walk-in cupboard with room for a double mattress on the floor, book shelves and a desk. Perfect. Twenty-six Lauriston Place became my home for the next four years.

At last I had somewhere to take a girl back to, and privacy and silence to practise Transcendental Meditation. I had learned the TM technique at the start of my first term and had been told that the practice was incompatible with the effects of dope, advice which I ignored at first, even turning up stoned to meditation sessions. But I soon realised it was true and consequently my dope smoking decreased. It was not difficult to get into a daily routine of two half-hour meditation sessions and before long I was beginning to see the benefits. It was taking me places deep inside myself, giving my body profound rest. I had been told not to expect dramatic spiritual experiences and these were not forthcoming. It was a gentle process. I particularly enjoyed the fact that the technique had been separated from its Hindu origins and had no obligatory belief system attached to it.

Robin, who had graduated with a Psychology degree and moved to a flat in Notting Hill Gate in London, had become very involved with the anti-psychiatry movement and in particular with the work of R.D. Laing and my namesake, David Cooper. Laing had established the Philadelphia Association and Robin started his own psychoanalytic training under its auspices, financing himself by doing odd jobs, gardening, and making and selling leather belts on Portobello Road. Although a couple of inches taller than my brother, I always felt in his shadow. He had a very sharp intellect, was articulate and academic, warm, compassionate and very funny. Naturally we fought, but I always felt Robin was there for me, and knew I could rely on him when necessary.

Robin and I would have regular discussions about the merits and demerits of meditation and psychoanalysis as paths to enlightenment, and as a result I was curious to find out more about his chosen way. When I returned to Edinburgh I contacted the Davidson Clinic, established in 1939 by Dr Winifred Rushforth. She herself interviewed me for my suitability to undergo psychoanalysis. Twice a week during term-time I went along to see Jean Neillands, an elderly analyst. No subject was off limits. I slept with a tape recorder by my bed to record dreams I would otherwise forget. I did most of the talking, she feeding back my words, always making me look deeper and examine my feelings, motives and reactions more closely. She let me away with nothing, and although sometimes the sessions were scary, I looked forward to them. I was not bothered at the time that she chain-smoked throughout the sessions, which were held in a small room with windows closed; in retrospect, it was not a healthy environment.

These sessions were inexpensive but they still needed funding, and although I was living on the maximum student grant available with no parental contribution, cash was a constant problem. Then I met Hugh Firth in the café of the university library one evening. His father, Raymond, was a social anthropologist whose books I had been studying as part of my course. It transpired that Hugh was a postgraduate doing research for his PhD on sleep, and he needed students to help with his experiments.

'What's involved?' I asked.

'Not a lot,' he replied. 'You commit to the series of experiments. You do not drink tea, coffee or alcohol, or take any drugs on the day of the experiment. You turn up at ten p.m., no more than twice a week; you will be out by eight a.m., with a hearty breakfast thrown in.' Then came the good bit.

'You will be paid five pounds a night, but only paid at the end of term.'

'What's the catch?' I wondered.

'You will not be asked to test for the effects of any drugs on sleep. But you will be woken up in different stages of sleep and asked to perform simple tests of memory.'

For a year, on and off, I was involved in a variety of experiments performed at the Royal Edinburgh Hospital in Morningside. Professor Ian Oswald, a national authority on sleep, was in overall charge of the unit. Horlicks funded one such experiment in an attempt to prove that the night-time drink improved sleep, but the results were inconclusive. The beauty of this for me was that not only was I being paid to sleep, but getting the money at the end of term when everyone else was broke. To put it in perspective, the grant worked out at £120 for a ten-week term which had to cover everything: food, rent, electricity, phone, drink, and any entertainment. I was getting around £100 cash in my pocket – easily enough to live on until the new term came around.

Sex, spirituality, socialism and song were the drivers of the day. These had to be worked around a fifth 's' – study, which sometimes seemed an intrusion. I had applied to do Sociology. Nothing I had done at school in any way motivated me to continue at university level. With three lectures and a tutorial a week, the work was not onerous, although getting out of bed after a late night, for a nine o'clock lecture was sometimes a struggle. I was also studying Social Anthropology, which interested me more. The third subject had been recommended by my Director of Studies, Frank Bechhofer.

'I suggest you do Metaphysics,' he said to the bespectacled, spotty-faced, long-haired youth in front of him. I had not a clue what it was but it sounded cool and I agreed. It was by far the hardest of the three courses and most of the time I did not understand the concepts, terminology or arguments, but Frank was right. It was very useful in providing a grounding in logical, rational thought and I am grateful to him for pointing me in this direction. By second year, however, I was more streetwise. I chose Architectural Studies as my outside subject, as I knew it involved only one lecture a week and three tutorials a term. The lectures, spent looking at slides of buildings from all over the world, learning about their creation, significantly enhanced my appreciation of foreign architecture.

Social Anthropology for first-year students was a popular course full of attractive young women, but one in particular caught my eye. Her infectious laughter lit up her face, that was part of her attraction, but she was also pretty, slender, and quite small with a mass of curly black hair. She was an Edinburgh girl called Jennie, and she was my first serious girlfriend at university.

She was interested and involved in the radical student political scene, and we would meet up at SocSoc meetings. She came from an impressive political heritage, her father being amongst the group of Scots who went out to fight Franco and his fascist regime in Spain. She had a flat in Montague Street but it was not long before she was spending more of her time in Lauriston Place. We went to a lot of concerts together and had some truly memorable nights in the Usher Hall with the Incredible String Band whose music caught the spirit of the times with their magical fusion of song and spirituality. Pink Floyd were at the height of their creative powers, their concerts major events, and I am glad I made the effort to see Nina Simone performing live. Although she is long dead, her music still captivates.

People came and went from number 26. The flat was owned by the university, and the flatmate whose job it was to collect rent from us was a Welshman called Steve Jones, who was doing his PhD in genetics. The kitchen was full of jam jars filled with snails and fruit flies. He would take some of us off to France in the summer months on snail gathering trips, where snails identified in previous excursions would be found and measured, and new ones marked for future research.

Then there was Boris, who had moved from a squat in West Adam Street when it was threatened with demolition. He shared a room in the basement with Pat Finlay, who had introduced me to the flat. They were both from Inverness and had known each other since school. Boris was not at university, nor did he have a fixed income, earning his living buying and selling cars and motorbikes. The hall, landing and corridors of the flat were always full of bits of engines. He also made a few trips to Amsterdam, returning with van-loads of leather coats and jackets and other trendy clothes which he sold to appreciative students. His real name was Donald Fraser and I suspect his striking blond hair and eyebrows earned him the 'Boris' soubriquet. His dog Mickey, a black Labrador, was his shadow in the streets and pubs of Edinburgh. Pat shared his enthusiasm for motorbikes and was able as anyone to strip one down and do a major repair.

John Clark was a third-year Philosophy student and the oldest person in the flat. Fiercely intelligent and with a very dry sense of humour, his downfall was alcohol. A Londoner by birth, he had already lost half of his liver, and he heeded his doctor's advice to stay off spirits, but drank instead copious amounts of Special Brew, the empties of which would pile up in large quantities besides Boris's bits of car and Steve's jars of fruit flies and snails.

Carolyn Evans, a Politics student, also lived in a basement room. 'Vaginal Powerhouse Testing Bay' she wrote in huge letters across the corridor wall, with an arrow pointing to her door. There was a fair amount of bed-hopping in the flat but I never found out if there was any basis of truth in her artwork.

Christine Glover was a Yorkshire lass, studying for an MSc in Sociology. She had a room next to mine on the ground floor. Blonde and tall, she was the matriarch of the flat into whose room we would often gravitate to drink, smoke dope and listen to music. She was a lovely, caring woman, always with a kind word and open heart. We were pretty lax around security and when a neighbour's kid wandered in to the house and stole a small amount of money, Christine was the first to defend her, saying it was our fault for putting temptation her way. There was a huge amount of socialism talked and debated in those days, but Christine was the only one amongst us who lived her own socialist truth. She was the one who came to pick me up on that cold winter night in Glencoe after I had been thrown out by my father.

Over the years many others came and went from the Lauriston Place flat. Some were there for a term or two and others, like

Steve Oldfield, made it their home. Originally from Birmingham, Steve had been working as the storeman for Scotland's major outdoor sports training centre, and somehow had ended up living in the flat. He joined Boris in the car business. He had left school at sixteen and had been fending for himself ever since. He was one of the first of the generation of hippies to make the overland trip to India and back and was full of stories. He remains one of the funniest raconteurs I have ever met. He had a beautiful girlfriend called Sue Rundle who lived in an adjacent flat and over the years there was much coming and going between the two residences. After Steve and Sue split up, she started seeing Robbie McMillan, a struggling actor who was often out of work and spent much of his time hanging around number 26. Large and loud, he could be very funny. Eventually he moved to London, changed his surname to Coltrane, and achieved fame as Rubeus Hagrid.

Colin Bowman was another regular visitor. When he needed somewhere to stay he cleared out what had originally been a wine cellar, piled high with junk for years. He built himself a platform bed with a desk underneath. Windowless and without ventilation, he was nevertheless pleased with his new-found home.

'We need to do something about these mice,' John Clark said to me one day, 'they are keeping me awake.' He was right, the place was overrun, and they were particularly active and noisy at night. I went out and bought a packet of mousetraps, but these vermin were clever and learned to extract the cheese without setting off the trap. Something more drastic was required. Although they had the run of the building, they seemed to concentrate behind the old kitchen range, which had not been lit in years. We found some kindling and coal and after some difficulty fired it up. It appeared that the chimney had also been blocked off, as smoke billowed out of the stove, from cracks in the wall, and then from behind blocked-off fireplaces in other rooms. We put the fire out, but the smoke lingered. Then came the mice. Hoards fled from the fireplace and ran straight outside. We whooped and hollered as we chased them on their way.

~

And then there were the visitors. I wasn't sure how I should address him. 'Ronnie' sounded too familiar, 'Dr Laing' or 'Sir' a bit too formal. In the end I tried all three, but had to resort to grabbing his collar and giving him a good shake to get any reaction at all. He had spread himself across the railway carriage, drunk. I had been commandeered to meet him at Waverley Station, and was disappointed that he did not emerge from the London train with the other passengers. I needed to get him out and sober enough to deliver a lecture at the university in a few hours' time. I grabbed his case and coat, jumped into a taxi and took him back to the flat.

R.D. Laing was a cult figure and 'New Age' hero who was attempting to transform the way mental illness, especially schizophrenia, was thought of and treated. A prolific author, his body of work was hugely influential, generating much interest and debate far beyond the bounds of his psychiatric profession. And here he was, drunk, in my flat, with a rapidly approaching appointment in front of a large audience. There were medical students around who helped me to sober him up and by the time he was due to take to the rostrum he was fine, although I found his speech disappointing, disjointed, with very slow delivery, and hard to follow. He stayed that night in the flat, and chatted warmly with us, refusing the offer of a joint, preferring his pipe and a dram.

For a time, there was a flurry of intense political activity in the flat. University student protests were virulent throughout Europe, and Edinburgh was no different. For some reason a whole bunch of students took over and occupied the university-run basement café of the David Hume Tower. What was normally rather drab and depressing was transformed into a lively, colourful place to hang out, and, for many, to sleep. Bands would perform, and girls would dance topless. A visiting theatre group, Les Tréteaux libres from that French hotbed of revolution, the Sorbonne, performed their political plays in the refectory. We managed to find them a floor to sleep on in Lauriston Place. The university largely ignored our sit-in and it was not long before we packed up our things and went home.

The next occupation was however much more serious and almost got me kicked out of university. It was discovered that the university was allowing South African companies, or companies committed to Apartheid, to recruit graduates through the Appointments Board in Buccleuch Place. A student protest quickly escalated into the building being taken over and occupied. Then the fun began. Files were opened and university activities were exposed. It seemed that the university had exceeded the limit for investments in the apartheid regime set by the Labour Government. Then we looked at the card indexes about individual students.

'Despite his working class background...' one started. 'Although from a Jewish family...' said another. A manual press was wheeled into the building, and whilst preserving people's anonymity, these practices were exposed. The story was picked up by the national press. We got word we were to be forcibly ejected in the early hours of the morning and all left before the police arrived.

Having been publicly humiliated, the university authorities were not going to let this go. Sympathetic sources warned us that they had the names of half a dozen students and were intent on expelling them. A petition was raised and also fifty-five of us signed a document admitting our involvement, in the belief that the authorities could not be seen to rusticate that number. We subsequently all appeared before the University Court, chaired by the Rector Ken Allsop, who thought we deserved medals. His was unfortunately a minority opinion and we received a suspended sentence for the rest of our time at university, to be rusticated if we stepped out of line again.

Some weeks later, the all-white South African rugby team were due to play Scotland at Murrayfield. An anti-apartheid protest was organised with the express intent of disrupting the match. This was part of a national 'Stop the Tour' campaign, details of which were to reach and give some encouragement to the imprisoned Nelson Mandela. The police presence was massive and many of us were dragged away from the demonstration, but the point was made to the South Africans that as long as apartheid prevailed they were not welcome. Congratulatory telegrams came flooding in to the Students' Union from celebrities and supporters from all over the world.

An important part of the anti-apartheid movement at the time was the boycotting of South African goods. I was in a small fruit and vegetable shop on Lauriston Place. A queue had built up behind me when it was my turn to be served. Amongst my purchases were some oranges and as the assistant was bagging them up for me I remembered the boycott.

'What sort of oranges are these?' I asked.

'Outspan,' came the reply.

'Oh, I am sorry, I can't have those, they are South African,' I said, feeling self-righteous.

A voice from a woman behind me in the queue rang out.

'Aye, son, quite right. Them dirty blacks handling the fruit, I wouldnae buy any myself.'

I was appalled.

Oh dear, I thought to myself, we do have a long way to go.

~

'Can I see your passport please, sir?'

Decades later, and I was standing in a queue at Gatwick to check in for a transatlantic flight. I was heading for the British Virgin Islands, but getting off at the American Virgin Islands and catching a connecting ferry. It was not long after the 9/11 attacks and security checks were stringent. This man was coming down the queue scanning passports on a hand-held machine.

He scanned mine, then asked, 'Is this your passport sir?'

'Yes, of course.'

'I'll be back in a minute,' he replied.

Twenty minutes later, he had not reappeared. I was next in line at the check-in, and getting anxious. Suddenly he was there, my passport in his outstretched hand.

'Is there a problem?' I asked.

'No,' came the reply, as he handed my passport back, with a suspicion of a smile. 'Just a misspent youth.'

~

The summer of 1969 came around and I was back in Yugoslavia, this time with Jennie. We had travelled through France and Italy, sometimes hitch-hiking, other times taking the train, sometimes staying in hostels, occasionally sleeping rough. We crossed the Aegean and landed in Patras, where a rich Greek who had seen us on the boat picked us up and drove us to Corinth. We hung out in the Pláka district in Athens, before heading back along the Dalmatian coast of Yugoslavia. Jennie was a great travelling companion, uncomplaining about the hardships of life on the road, and we got on very well, despite there being no respite from each other's company. Our friendship deepened. One evening we were picked up outside Sarajevo by three local men, and we soon regretted getting into the car. They drove us round for hours, refusing to let us out. Their manner became unpleasant and they started asking if we were married. Jennie moved her mother's wedding ring onto her fourth finger, though of course this would have made no difference if they indeed were up to no good. At one point they tried to separate us, but after about three hours they dropped us at a remote petrol station in the early hours of the morning. We found out later that they had driven us through our actual destination over two hours before. In the morning Jennie realised her mother's wedding ring had slipped off her finger. She was inconsolable.

Back in Edinburgh, cracks were appearing in our relationship. TM was becoming an increasingly important part of my life and Jennie showed no interest in learning. Our ways amicably parted. We had felt a lot of love for each other, and this was a new experience for me. Before Jennie, no-one had ever said they loved me. It would never have occurred to Tony or Ursula to say that to their children, and indeed when I accused them of not loving me when I was a child, Tony beat me for my insolence.

Ursula had kept Tony's letters to her, written just after they were married, when his search for work took him away from her. As one might expect they were full of passion and desire, but throughout the time I knew him, with one exception, I never experienced any expression of love or warmth to my mother or to Jo, Robin or myself.

Although he worked hard to provide for us all, he was just not capable of giving the emotional strength that any growing child or young adult needs. And Ursula was no better. There was a temporary respite from her cold frame of mind, which came about when Ursula went on a cycling holiday in France with Jo and was knocked down by a passing motorcyclist. She sustained a severe head injury and spent several days in hospital in France. The time I spent with Tony in this crisis revealed a different side of him. I was amazed to see him so emotional. He cried when told that Ursula was conscious and showing signs of recovery, and was visibly thrilled when she eventually came back to this country by air ambulance to be admitted to a hospital in Birmingham.

Ursula had undergone an even more dramatic transformation.

'Oh David, dear David, how wonderful to see you. How kind of you to go to all this trouble. I am so sorry for causing all these problems. You have all been so fantastic, I am so grateful to you.'

Jo and I looked at each other in amazement. Who was this loving, caring, sensitive soul? The brain injury had fundamentally changed her character. However her recovery was total, both mental and physical, and it was not long before the cold and critical personality we knew so well, returned. Tony and Ursula had not provided me with the most useful foundation for developing my own loving relationships. There was certainly plenty of material to work with in psychoanalysis and the other therapeutic processes I dabbled with. However, my heart was increasingly leaning towards TM. The benefits I felt from practising the technique regularly convinced me that the process would dissolve any psychological impasses created by my upbringing. I became increasingly involved with the TM movement and in early 1970 began the long process of learning how to teach the technique to others.

I found work as a temporary assistant school janitor, helping with maintenance jobs which could not be done during term-time. Over the Easter break I worked at Boroughmuir Secondary and for the summer I was to replace the janitor at Corstorphine Primary, where the permanent janitor was on prolonged sick leave. School was still in when I started, and there had been a headline in the *Edinburgh Evening News* about the unacceptable length of hair of a male teacher in Fife. Someone from Corstorphine wrote in, saying, 'If you think this teacher's hair is too long, you should come and see our jannie!' The first I knew of this was a reporter and photographer turning up at my office in the school. They chatted and took a couple of photos and I thought no more about it.

A couple of days later I was on my way home and I saw the *Edinburgh Evening News* billboard with the headline 'Corstorphine's Hippie Janitor'. I nearly fell off my bike! My photo was on the front page with the caption 'Can you guess what this youth does for a living?'. Inside there was another photo and a half-page article. But the job paid well and financed the rest of the summer. I hitch-hiked down to the Isle of Wight concert, a three-day event which included what was to be the last public appearance by Jimi Hendrix. I was so tired by the time he came on in the early hours of day three, that I lay down and slept through his entire performance.

CHAPTER FIVE

On the Road Again

In 1970 I first met Maharishi Mahesh Yogi. I had embarked upon a Transcendental Meditation teacher-training programme in Kössen, a small village high in the Austrian Alps, where he was holding a month-long course which I needed to attend as part of the process of becoming a TM teacher. There were a few hundred people attending, mostly young, from all over the world. Until then these courses had been held in his ashram in India, where The Beatles had famously spent a few weeks. Now Maharishi had to come to the West to conduct the training himself. We would meet with him three times a day, and spend the rest of the time alone in our individual rooms in local houses in prolonged meditation sessions. The meetings were informal, and we could ask him what we liked. There was a Canadian at the microphone with a massive amount of hair that looked like it was exploding out of his head. He had beads, sandals, cut-off jeans and a Grateful Dead t-shirt. He was not untypical of the audience. Maharishi interrupted him as he was asking a question:

'You are going to have to do something about your appearance,' he said. 'If you are going to represent me and this ancient tradition of Vedic wisdom, you will have no credibility looking like that.'

The Canadian stared at Maharishi, sitting full lotus on the settee with his long black hair and beard, beads and sandals.

'But you are the biggest freak in the room!' he replied. For a second there was a shocked silence, then Maharishi burst into laughter, something he was prone to do.

Nevertheless, that was the start of a dress code for TM teachers. Hair became shorter, and eventually jackets and ties were mandatory when teaching. In early March 1971 my training culminated in a twelve-week residential course held in Majorca where Maharishi had taken over a group of out-of-season hotels. There were several hundred trainee TM teachers, again from all over the world. This was far more intense than anything I had experienced before. In many ways, Maharishi was learning from the experience of teaching such a large group as he went along. We were, in a real sense, his guinea pigs. There was, for instance, no limit on the amount of meditation we could do. We were expected to be at all evening meetings with Maharishi. Simultaneous translations would be going on in different sections of the vast dining room for those who did not speak English. Other than that, the expectation was that we practised TM as much as we could in the time that was left from the meetings and eating. Around twelve hours a day for the duration of the course were spent deep in meditation, broken only for short spells of yoga and breathing exercises. Then weeks of silence were imposed on us, where we could only talk if asking Maharishi a question. This was not a hardship, however, as these extended meditations took you so deep into your being that soon it became almost too much of an effort to communicate.

Not only were we getting Maharishi's undivided attention on a daily basis, we were also getting an extraordinary understanding of the processes of personal evolution and growth direct from an enlightened master. I felt privileged to be there and would not have missed it for the world.

Not everybody enjoyed it. For some, the result of gaining such profound physical and mental rest produced strange physical side effects as deeply rooted stresses left their nervous system. This could cause involuntary physical twitches. A corner in the dining hall was set aside for these dramatic 'unstressers'. Stories would circulate of others for whom the whole thing had become too much, who had either left of their own accord or been thrown out.

I celebrated my twenty-first birthday in Majorca on this course, and a short time later was given the best present I could have dreamt of. After a private audience with Maharishi I was given the knowledge and permission to teach TM to others.

~

'Do I know you? Have we met before?' my tutor asked when I walked into his tutorial soon after my return to Edinburgh. I had not been seen in the department, and had some serious catching up to do. There were no end of term exams in third year, which is just as well as I would certainly have failed them. Instead we were supposed to research the dissertation which was a significant part of the final assessment for an honours degree.

That summer I stayed on the island of Lismore in a cottage with no electricity, drawing the water I needed from a nearby well. Occasionally friends came to stay but mostly I was on my own. I spent much of my time as a willing but unpaid labourer helping out a neighbouring farmer, learning to drive a tractor, plough a field and clip sheep.

My relationships with women at the time were beginning to fall into a pattern. Either I was more keen on them than they me, or vice versa. I couldn't achieve an equal balance. In my fourth year I was with Kate, an English Literature student from Hemel

Hempstead, who I felt was a real soul-mate, but she did not feel the same. Nevertheless, we spent a holiday together on Kerrera and she was the first girlfriend I introduced to my parents. We were supportive to each other as we worked for our final exams, but had very different plans for our lives. After university, she moved back down to England. I had found employment with the farmer who owned the Isle of Muck, utilising skills picked up the previous summer, but at the last minute changed my mind and headed instead to North America.

I flew into Toronto from Glasgow on a British Universities North America Club flight, in an ancient student-filled plane that rattled and shook its way across the Atlantic. Toronto was hot and humid and I did not stay long. I hitch-hiked down to London, Ontario, where the Buckland family kindly took me in for a few days. Robert Buckland, a Canadian colleague of my brother, had suggested I stopped off with his parents to acclimatise myself to a new continent. It was my first experience of North American hospitality, a total stranger being taken in and treated with great warmth and generosity. It was something I was to appreciate many times in the next few months.

I walked into America at Sarnia crossing a bridge over the St Clair River which separates these two vast nations. Hitch-hiking was easy. I opted for a quieter coastal route, up through Flint, to Saginaw and along the west shore of Lake Huron to Rogers City, eventually crossing a long bridge at Mackinaw, and back into Canada at Sault Sainte Marie. The intention was to hitch-hike Highway Seventeen, the Trans-Canada Highway, to Vancouver, a little under two thousand miles away, but I had an immediate problem.

I had been warned by travellers that the route between Sault Sainte Marie and Thunder Bay, some five hundred miles of lake, trees and little else, was notoriously difficult to hitch-hike across. Right in the middle was a town called Wawa, the only place of any size or significance but which was still very small. Stories of hitch-hikers getting stuck there were rife. Some got employment in local bars at night and tried to hitch-hike out during the day. In an ingenious scheme to make use of all this youthful energy, literally going nowhere, in 1971 the federal government set up the Wawa Drop-In Project or the Big Dig, an archaeological field camp. Fortunately I did not have to resort to finding work, as after refusing a few shorter lifts, an ex-pat Scot from Fort William stopped for me. Although staying the night in Wawa, he was continuing the next day to Thunder Bay where he dropped me off in the early afternoon. Cross-continent hitch-hiking was common, and I would leapfrog fellow travellers on the long road west. Some small towns had created tented accommodation especially for us, and with a bed, a shower and something to eat for a couple of dollars they were welcome refuges. The Vietnam War was raging, and many draft dodgers had fled to Canada to avoid the fighting. Some had served one term of duty and were refusing to return for a second. I was woken one night by terrible screaming coming from an adjacent tent. It sounded as though someone was being tortured, and in a way they were. It transpired it was a Vietnam veteran, whose nightly sleep was ravaged by nightmares from his war experiences. The US army authorities had refused him help, and when they tried to send him back he went on the run. It seemed Canada stretched on forever. Ontario, Manitoba, Saskatchewan, the States rolled by as did the days, slowly and with little change of scenery. Eventually the hazy blue outline of the Rockies appeared in the far distance, and a day later they appeared no nearer. But the place names were getting more romantic and evocative of the indigenous population – Moose Jaw, Swift Current, Medicine Hat – and then slowly the gradient increased and I was climbing, the days getting cooler with the altitude. Place names began to reflect the Scottish roots of the early pioneers of the country. I

the car was automatic, and I soon got the hang of it. I drove for hours, slowing down to a crawl to pass through the checkpoint for farm produce at the Californian State boundary, then accelerating back onto the fast lane. I was heading for a fruit-farming commune near the small town of Winters in the Sacramento Valley. The directions were good and it was not hard to find, at the end of a dirt track a few miles out of town. I stopped in the farm yard, woke up the occupants and told them how to get back to the Interstate. It was the first time I had driven a car.

I had heard about the place from Pete, an American student at Edinburgh University. He had prepared the way and I was half-expected. Earl was the first to greet me, a tall, full-bearded man with long greying hair, wearing dungarees, boots and a torn t-shirt.

'Howdy, man,' he said as he led me into one of the buildings. It was blisteringly hot and the proffered ice-cold drink was welcome. He told me about the commune.

'I don't own the land,' he explained, 'but the guy who does lets us use it as we want, so long as we give him some of what we grow. Food and accommodation are free, but we're not paid. We sell some of what we grow from the side of the highway, but we distribute most of it free in the poorest parts of Sacramento and Oakland. Any income is put back into the farm. Once a week we take a trip into Berkeley with a truckload of fruit for the Black Panthers to distribute locally. And it's totally organic; we use no fertilisers or chemicals at all. You are welcome here as long as you like.'

Earl and his wife Wendy, were effectively in charge of the place. A gentle giant of a man, he decided on work priorities and what crops went where. There was a core of about twelve people, friends and supporters dropping in, sometimes only for a weekend. The work was varied. Some days were spent ploughing but most of the time I was picking melons, the main crop. You had to test each melon's ripeness before breaking it off its stem. This being an organic farm the local bugs flourished, especially black widow spiders, which could give you a very nasty bite. The technique was to roll the melon over with your foot; the spider underneath would then scuttle away. During my time there, no one was bitten, but I was the only one to wear boots and gloves, too much of a coward to brave a spider bite.

We took it in turns to drive to the nearest highway to sell the fruit from a roadside stall. Whatever the task, the days ended in the late afternoon with everyone heading down to the creek for a skinny dip in the cooling waters.

One weekend I was asked along on the Oakland run to drop fruit off with the Black Panthers, a hugely influential black movement organisation of the late 1960s. Their leader, Bobby Seale, had just been released from prison after serving four years for incitement to riot at the Democrat Convention in Chicago in 1968. At his trial he interrupted proceedings so often he was eventually bound and gagged, to the lasting disgrace of the American system of justice.

By the time of his release, the Black Panther movement had embarked on a programme to 'feed the youth and feed the revolution', initially concentrating on the black children gathered at the Concord Baptist Church near Berkeley, which is where the commune was dropping off the food. I was hoping Bobby Seale would be there but of course he was not.

That evening we were staying with a group of Berkeley students, friends of one of the people on the farm. We decided to go for a late night swim. This involved climbing over a garden fence of a nearby old folks' home, stripping off and tiptoeing stark naked behind a group of residents to get to the outside pool where we silently swam for a half hour before returning. The residents were a bunch of old guys who were too engrossed watching soft porn on the TV to notice a bunch of naked people, including some beautiful women, parading behind them.

I was made to feel very welcome on the commune. I loved being there and felt very much part of the extended family. But I also wanted to see more of the country. After a couple of weeks I decided to take off for a while and see the places I wanted to see. In late July I left for San Francisco, where I did a few days sightseeing, before heading off to Lake Tahoe and on through Nevada and Utah, stopping at the South Rim of the Grand Canyon before crossing the Colorado River, past the Painted Desert, eventually arriving in Albuquerque, New Mexico. After staying with some friends there I moved on again to El Paso, crossed into Mexico to Juárez, then back to Santa Fe, before accepting the offer of a lift all the way back to Berkeley. Two weeks after leaving the farm I was back.

Days turned into weeks. Life was idyllic. Working on the fields or selling at the roadside stall during the day, relaxing with the group, often round a fire and barbeque in the evening, we rarely went inside. There was a meteor shower forecast one night, and I wandered off with my sleeping mat away from the firelight to fall asleep watching the show. Crossing a dried-out stream-bed in the dark and with no torch, I heard a noise which made me freeze. I had seen enough cowboy films to recognise the sound of a rattlesnake. I could not tell what direction the sound was coming from. I stood on one leg as if to give the snake less of a target to hit, then started speaking to it.

'Go away nice snake,' I pleaded. Silence. I decided to try another tack, picked up some stones and threw them in all directions, making lots of noise.

Still silence. I can't stand here all night, I thought. Fearfully I carried on, found the flat bit of field I was aiming for, lay down and eventually slept.

~

Earl and Wendy offered to pay my Greyhound Bus fare to New York if I stayed longer, but I decided to take my chances hitch-hiking back. I drove down to Berkeley with another load of fruit and set off the next morning to hitch a ride on University Avenue, along with about thirty other hitch-hikers going to destinations all over the continent. I had been there a couple of hours when a VW van drove by slowly. Five minutes later it came by again. The couple inside were assessing potential companions for their journey to New York. They stopped and chatted for a while, and my agreement to share petrol costs clinched it. They were in no hurry. We stopped off at Salt Lake City, then Yellowstone National Park, on through Wyoming, South Dakota, stopping at the Badlands and Mount Rushmore, eating in local cafés and sleeping in the van. I got them to drop me off in Cleveland where I stayed with friends for a couple of days. Four days later I was standing in Manhattan beside one of the huge pillars supporting the Brooklyn Bridge. It was dark, it was raining, funds were getting low, I had nowhere to go.

I sheltered in a phone box and took stock of my situation. I went through my address book but it was devoid of New York contacts. In my wallet I found a business card with an address in New Rochelle, a wealthy New York suburb. But who was this Theodore Greene, his name embossed in copperplate script? Then I remembered and dialled his number.

'Mr Greene?'

'Yes, that's me, can I help?'

'This might seem a little strange, but please don't hang up. You were on holiday in Scotland last summer?'

'Yes, that's right. What's this about?'

'In a place called Glencoe you went into a shop and bought a whole pile of things, and spoke at some length to the owner, a man with big bushy whiskers, wearing a kilt.'

'Yes, I remember him, a real Highland gentleman.'

I resisted the temptation to say he was English.

'You gave that man your business card and said that if ever he or his family were in New York, they should look you up. Well I am his son and I am in New York.'

'Wow, that's great. Do you need somewhere to stay?' A couple of hours later I was sitting in the garden of his mansion drinking wine with Ted Greene, city councillor and businessman. He lived with his wife Jacqueline and their daughter Debbie. The maid was instructed to make up my room. I had landed on my feet.

Ted was a solidly built, slightly overweight man of about sixty, a couple of inches under six foot, with thinning grey hair swept back over a large head. He was bright, articulate, and spoke with a strong New York accent. A Republican, he lived for politics and was an avid collector of antiques. He was a generous host.

'I have a favour to ask of you,' he said over breakfast the next morning. 'I need to be in two places at once today, but now you can be at one of them on my behalf.'

I looked bemused.

'I'll explain on the way.'

He had a choice of four cars in the garage, each magnificent. He chose the convertible Audi. The roof slid back as we exited the drive.

'There are a couple of antique auctions on today at the same time, in different parts of the city. I am going to one and I am going to ask you to bid on my behalf at the other.'

My destination turned out to be an elegant, upmarket auction house full of expensive suits. I stood out like a sore thumb.

Ted gave me instructions to buy the items he wanted irrespective of the price.

It took about an hour for the first item on my list to come under the hammer.

'Lot fifty-one,' the auctioneer announced. 'This wonderful London-made long case clock in perfect condition. Who will start the bidding at five thousand dollars?'

I decided to bide my time and waited until the bidding was between two individuals. One was becoming more hesitant, and dropped out at $12,500. The remaining bidder's smile disappeared as I raised my hand. A couple of minutes later I had bought the piece for $14,000. Exactly the same happened a few minutes later. This time it was an old music machine Ted was after, complete with large metal music disks, beautifully inlaid and in perfect working order. I spent another $20,000.

These were by far the most expensive items in the sale and I was relieved that Ted had cleared it with the auctioneer that I would be bidding on his behalf. People came up to me assuming I was some sort of eccentric millionaire, and I was enjoying this illusion until Ted came in and broke the spell, paid for the goods and arranged for their delivery. He was delighted with his purchases.

Over breakfast the next morning he outlined his plans for the day.

'We are going to a private airstrip,' he said. 'I have something I need to do and do not want to do it alone.'

In a different car we headed out of town, and in half an hour pulled into the car park of a private flying club. We were expected and were led out onto the tarmac to a waiting twin-engine aircraft.

'Hold this, will you?' Ted asked as he clambered in beside the pilot. He handed me a small cardboard box. I climbed in behind him. We took off and were soon circling above Manhattan. Ted slid open a window and from the box took out a jar, removed the top, and emptied the contents over the city. The ashes streamed out behind us for a second or two, and then were gone.

'That was my father,' Ted explained. 'That was totally illegal, but what the hell, it's what he would have wanted.'

Ted's daughter Debbie, who was a few years older than me, was chatty and friendly. Ted encouraged us to go out together for evening drives around into Manhattan, visiting the occasional bar and club. Ted usually stuffed a bundle of dollar bills into my hand as we were leaving to finance these city expeditions.

There was one thing I needed to do on my own. When I was sixteen I had bought my first record. I had saved up a long time for it and it was my pride and joy. I remember playing it endlessly to an unappreciative audience of school friends. The record was *Highway 61 Revisited* by Bob Dylan. I have been a little obsessed with the man and his music ever since.

Rumours were circulating amongst Dylan fans of the existence of tapes of rare and wonderful material. There was a man who lived in Bleecker Street, downtown Manhattan, a self-styled Dylanologist. I was determined to meet him.

We spoke on the phone and Alan Jules Weberman invited me round to listen to his archive material. He had an armoured entrance area, tear gas canisters, and video surveillance, which made me think he must be paranoid. Dressed in striped trousers and a New York Giants t-shirt, with bushy hair and an unshaven face, he talked very fast and pretty much nonstop. Clearly, he thrived on nervous energy. His house was filled with material relating to Dylan. Weberman made a living of sorts as a freelance music journalist, but he was embarking on teaching courses on Dylan and setting up what he called the Dylan Liberation Front with an aim of persuading the artist to return to his political songwriting roots. He later took to rummaging through Dylan's garbage cans, eventually harassing him to the extent that Dylan was to beat him up in a New York street.

He offered me a copy of a tape with some rare unrecorded material on it and I arranged to drop by the following day to pick it up.

It turned out to be an interesting afternoon and early evening. Weberman had only just come in when I arrived. After making some coffee he excused himself, saying he was going to have a shower.

I was sitting in his kitchen when the phone rang.

'Could you get that?' Weberman shouted through.

'Hi, is A.J. there?' asked the voice on the phone.

'Yes, but he's in the shower,' I replied. 'Can I take a message?'

'No, it's OK, I'll ring back.' The caller hesitated and then asked, 'You are not from around here?'

I told him I was from Scotland.

'I used to have holidays in Scotland as a kid,' the stranger replied, 'it's a lovely country, I sometimes wish I could live a simple life there as a fisherman on the west coast.'

We chatted for a while and I noticed that his accent had a slight American edge, but the basic brogue was English.

'You're not from here either?' I asked.

'No, I'm from Liverpool. I've been living here for a while, trying to get my green residency card.'

Even then, I had no idea who I was talking to. Weberman appeared and took the phone out of the room. He was back a few minutes later.

'That was John Lennon,' he said. 'He's giving a concert next week in aid of a charity for handicapped children. It's part of what he needs to do to get his green card. He wants his pals in the front rows and he's throwing a party afterwards. You're invited.'

'Far out! Fantastic! When is it?'

'Next Saturday night.'

My flight home was on Saturday afternoon. The ticket was non-refundable and non-exchangeable. I had just enough cash to get me through the next few days. This was a once-in-a-lifetime opportunity I would have to miss.

CHAPTER SIX

Poets, Pundits and Prisoners of War

Back in Edinburgh I moved into the new TM centre, a top-floor flat in Buccleuch Place, and started teaching the technique full time. Demand was constant and I was teaching the four-day course and follow-up meetings in all the Scottish university cities. Being shy by nature, it was daunting to have to face sometimes large audiences, but Maharishi had taught me well and my confidence grew; what I was teaching clearly worked.

The centre was a three-bedroom, top-floor Georgian flat with views over the Meadows and beyond to the Pentland Hills south of the city. At group meetings every Wednesday evening, when we would meditate, listen to a Maharishi tape or watch a video, technology that was just becoming commercially available. Soon after I moved into the flat, a woman who was new to the city came to one of these meetings; she was to play a significant role in my life.

Carolyn Becket had come up to the Edinburgh Festival, fallen in love with Edinburgh, and decided to stay. She quickly found employment as secretary to the University Press Office. With shoulder-length blonde hair and a dimple, she was attractive, fun and intelligent. We enjoyed each other's company and when a room became vacant in the flat, she moved in. It was not long before we were a couple.

Carolyn threw herself heart and soul into helping me run the centre. When I was not teaching we would head out to the country for the weekend, visiting friends in Fife or Kerrera, or going for long walks in the Pentlands or the beach at Gullane if we were staying at home. We tried to be back every Sunday evening in time for the University Film Society, which would take over the whole Odeon Cinema just around the corner from the flat.

I could see us settling down, but Carolyn had never made any secret of her continuing relationship with Adrian, her childhood boyfriend, who now lived in Yugoslavia. Torn between the two of us, she would write to him regularly and spend her longer holidays with him. She was very honest with me about her predicament, and although Adrian and I gradually learned a lot about each other, it would be years before we met.

Carolyn and I decided one summer to explore the north and west of Scotland together, and headed off to Orkney. While camping on farmland on the main island, we borrowed ancient bikes from the farmer and attempted to cycle round the island and whatever direction we went in, it felt like we were always going uphill into wind and rain.

I had been seasick on the way over from Scrabster, but the sail back to the mainland was calm. We hitch-hiked across the top of the country, and travelled slowly down the West Coast, eventually arriving on Islay in the dark, pitching the tent on the first piece of grass we stumbled across after disembarking from the ferry. Not till morning did we realise that we were on the middle of a traffic roundabout at the entrance to Port Ellen, the main town. We were on our way to see Captain Graham Donald, a self-taught Gaelic scholar, linguist, bon vivant, eccentric and colourful character, who had written about the connections he had found between the Gaelic language and the language of the Etruscan civilisation of Italy. But he had another more contemporary and fascinating story to tell. He lived with his wife in a modern bungalow at the south end of the island and spent most of his waking hours in his extensive garden shed, at the back of which was a large gravestone – which turned out to be his own.

'I am fed up with seeing nonsense written on other people's gravestones,' he explained, resting his feet on it, 'so I have had it done. All that needs to be added is the date of my death! It works fine as a table as well.'

My eye was caught by what appeared to be part of a wing from a wrecked plane hanging on the wall, in the middle of which was the clear marking of a black cross.

Graham Donald saw me looking at it and started telling his story.

'During the war I was in the Royal Observer Corps, stationed in East Renfrewshire. Pretty boring really, not a lot going on. But all that changed one night in May 1941. I got a call from an agitated shepherd who told me a German plane had crash-landed near his isolated cottage, and the pilot was sitting in his kitchen. Sure enough, when I arrived there was an airman sitting drinking a cup of tea.'

The pilot had parachuted and his injuries were minor. He was taken to the Home Guard base, then to the local police station. A fluent German speaker, Captain Donald, then a major, conducted the initial interview.

When asked why he was here, the man identified himself as Alfred Horn. He said he had an important message for the Duke of Hamilton and would talk only to him.

'I knew that Horn was a common name in Bavaria, but this man had more of a Hamburg accent, so I asked him where he had been born and raised, and something about the way he answered made me sure he was lying to me.'

'Then I made a chance remark – I pointed out that he had

the same initials as his Fuhrer. The reaction was so strong that I knew there was something strange going on, and began to think the impossible. Could this man in front of me be the Deputy Fuhrer of the Third Reich, Rudolph Hess?'

Keeping his discovery to himself, Captain Donald instructed the policeman on duty to leave the prisoner in a locked cell and allow no-one else in. He then found a phone and dialled Whitehall. It was three a.m.

'I need to speak to the Prime Minister, please put me through.'

'Impossible, sir, but there are staff who can deliver a message in the morning—'

'What I have is for his ears only. It is of national importance, he needs to hear this right now.'

After much arguing, he was passed up the chain of command and eventually an unmistakable voice came on the line.

'This better be bloody important, or you are history. Who have you got up there, Hitler?'

'No, sir. Hess, sir.'

'Bloody hell!' said Churchill, 'Are you sure? Don't go near him again; we'll have people up with you in the morning.'

~

Occasionally we would have someone very senior in the TM organisation come up to Scotland, and once Maharishi's right-hand man came to Edinburgh for a weekend. He was an impressive figure, well over six-feet, with a huge black beard and hair which tumbled down the back of the traditional white silk dhoti worn by Indian holy men. Devendra had trained as a lawyer before giving himself up to the search for enlightenment and service to Maharishi. Our paths were to later cross again in a very different set of circumstances.

It was announced that Maharishi himself would visit

Edinburgh at the end of a tour of European capital cities. It was a mammoth task to organise – a conference, accommodation for about a hundred delegates, venue, press, transport, guest speakers, invitations – the list seemed endless.

I called up the Lothian Region Parks Department with a cheeky request I thought had no chance of being fulfilled and was put through to one of the superintendents.

'You know that large floral plaque, the bed of flowers that sits halfway up The Mound? Well, there is a very important Indian guru arriving in the city next weekend and I thought it would be nice to honour his presence by having the letters TM written in flowers.'

The reply was unexpected and memorable.

'What colour, sir?'

'We should thank them for that.' Maharishi said as he was driven to the Assembly Hall to address the conference the following week.

The visit was covered on television and in the national press. It was the end of the tour and Maharishi was not due back in Switzerland for another few days.

'How would you like to see some of the country?' I suggested to him one evening. He was intrigued by the idea. I booked a bus and accommodation for the following three days. On our way through Glencoe I pointed out my parents' place.

'We'll go see them,' said Maharishi and the bus emptied into the Craft Shop. I took Maharishi into the adjacent house to meet my parents and he stayed chatting to them for an hour before we moved on. They were hugely impressed and came up to Fort William on the following evenings to spend a little more time in his company.

Maharishi first came out of India to the West in 1959. He died, aged ninety, in 2008. Many millions had come to meditation through him, in over a thousand centres, in more than fifty countries. He spent the vast bulk of his life in Europe and in all his time in this continent, the house in Glencoe was the only private house he ever entered.

It was one of several close encounters I had with the man. Whilst training, I would see him every afternoon and evening as he answered questions on anything anyone wanted to ask. He would address the entire course, maybe two or three hundred participants, and talk, sometimes for hours, about TM, personal growth and Hindu philosophy. He was a man filled with joy, always sparkling with humour and fun. I found these sessions inspirational. I felt privileged to be receiving this knowledge from an enlightened master. However, he remained a distant figure, unapproachable unless you were part of the small group of people who looked after him. This changed after I became a teacher of the technique and occasionally I would be in a room with two or three others and Maharishi. At first I felt awestruck and nervous, but later I was able to relax and enjoy his company, sharing stories and laughs.

He looked every bit the guru. He always sat cross-legged on deerskin on a settee covered by a white sheet. There was an abundance of fresh flowers wherever he was. His attire never altered, always a white silk dhoti covering his body, with a cashmere shawl over his shoulders in the winter. When I first met him his hair was mostly black and he had a long beard. He went grey and when I last saw him, both his hair and beard were completely white.

The most unusual encounter happened in Seelisberg, Switzerland, where Maharishi and the organisation surrounding him had been based for a number of years. There were a couple of hundred people in the room and we were watching Maharishi decide on the correct artwork for some new course material. He caught my eye and indicated that I should approach. Wondering what this was about, I went onto the stage and stood slightly to

Left: The author's parents on their wedding day, December 1941.

Below: Loch Coull House, outside Tarland, Aberdeenshire.

From the celebrity enclosure, Blackbushe 'Picnic', September 1978. On the right you can see the broken wall being repaired.

Poet Allen Ginsberg on the ferry crossing from Mull to Iona in 1973.

A game of buzkashi, Kabul stadium, autumn 1978. The nearest rider is carrying the dead goat.

The standing Buddha statues of Bamiyan, northern Afghanistan, later reduced to rubble by the mujahedeen.

Children help to work the fields, Northern Afghanistan.

Crossing the Shandur Pass, Northern Pakistan, winter 1978.

Left: Baltit, Hunza, Northern Pakistan. Right: The author at the Annapurna Sanctuary, Nepal.

A Tibetan refugee, Boudhanath, Kathmandu valley, Nepal.

Jyotirmath, Uttarakhand State, Northern India.

Left: Guru Dev, Brahamanda Saraswati, teacher of Maharishi Mahesh Yogi.
Right: Devendra on the path around Arunchala, Tirivannamalai, South India.

Face Piercing, Penang, Malaysia.

Left: An Orang Utang, wild and free in its natural habitat, Northern Sumatra.
Right: A typical Toba Batak house.

The author's host and family, central Samosir Island, Lake Toba, Sumatra.

Restored from a ruin in 1968, Crafts & Things, Glencoe, is now a successful business.

one side of him. He pointed to the settee and I sat down beside him.

For the next fifteen minutes I sat there whilst he carried on with what he had been doing. Eventually he turned to me and whispered, 'Look at these weak people, all dependent on my strength.'

I was dumbstruck. I had no idea how I should react. But I got a sense of his loneliness and said nothing. As the meeting broke up, Maharishi remembered why he had asked me up there and asked if I could drive some visiting Indian dignitaries around several European capitals. I found someone else who had the time and inclination to do this. Days later Maharishi sent most of the people in the room, many of whom were American, back home to their own countries.

As I was running the centre and teaching TM across Scotland full-time, my basic living expenses were covered. For many of my colleagues in the country in a similar situation this was sufficient, but although I loved what I was doing, I was aware that I did not want to be doing it forever and started to consider a more conventional career. I had enjoyed being an undergraduate, but a second-class honours degree in Social Anthropology was not going to open up doors of opportunity. I looked at several different options, but was left with the feeling of standing at a multi-junction crossroads, with each enticing path guarded by an open gate. As I ventured through one gate and looked back the others were closing, and I hurried back to the point of indecision where all the avenues of possibility were open again.

Partly as a result of this indecision, partly through laziness, I decided to go back to university and embark upon a two-year postgraduate course which would result in a Social Work qualification. This was an enticing prospect for all the wrong reasons. Much of the academic work I had already covered in my first degree. Edinburgh Corporation, the precursor to Lothian Regional Council, was sponsoring graduates to complete the training with the proviso that graduates worked for them for at least two years. I was going to be a salaried student with an undemanding workload for the foreseeable future.

The flat in Buccleuch Place had one major disadvantage as a TM Centre. It was at the top of eighty-four steps, and for some of the elderly meditators this was proving a problem. The perfect alternative came up in Victoria Street, which winds its way from George IV Bridge down to the Grassmarket. A large flat had come onto the market. Its purchase meant that the Buccleuch Place flat would have to be sold, but the owners agreed to sell to me – now that I was on a salary I could borrow the necessary money. Seven thousand pounds for a three-bedroom flat in the heart of Georgian Edinburgh Southside seemed a lot then, but with a hundred per cent mortgage, the property became mine, and home for the next thirteen years.

The postgraduate course flew by. Holidays were largely spent at residential meditation courses or on Kerrera, where my sister Jo and her husband Alan and their daughters had returned to run a farm they had leased on the island. One summer I decided to head off to Iona, where I planned to camp at the north end for a week or two. I took the train to Glasgow and had to change stations for the Oban train from Queen Street. I was running late. In those days there was no corridor linking compartments, so there was no possibility of leaving a carriage until the train stopped. I ran down the platform, with doors banging and whistles blowing, looking for the emptiest compartment I could find. Right at the end of the train there was one with only two people inside. I opened the door and had barely sat down before we were moving.

I took stock of my travelling companions. One was a scrawny young man who did not catch my eye and responded to my 'hello' with a monosyllabic grunt. His companion looked more dramatic, with large dark-rimmed glasses, long black hair and a greying beard, wearing denim dungarees and sandals. He looked at least twenty years older than me. He had a bandaged leg and his crutches were by his side. He met my eye and responded to my greeting with an American accent. I fished around in my rucksack and pulled out the book I was reading, a newly published biography of Jack Kerouac, whose work I had been devouring over the last six months. I settled and started reading where I had left off on the train through from Edinburgh. The chapter was describing Kerouac's relationship with Allen Ginsberg, the other founding father of the American Beat generation and the counterculture that was to follow. Ginsberg was a friend of Bob Dylan's, and his epic poem 'Howl' denounced what he saw as the destructive forces of capitalism and conformity in American culture. I could even remember the first stanza:

I saw the best minds of my generation destroyed by madness, starving hysterical, naked,
dragging themselves through the negro streets at dawn, looking for an angry fix...

The man with the glasses cleared his throat and I glanced up. Looking at him again, I realised that he actually looked a bit like Ginsberg. Correction: a lot like him. Bloody hell! I thought to myself, it can't be! But curiosity got the better of me.

'You going to Oban?' I asked.

'Yes,' he replied, 'then catching the ferry to Iona.'

I smiled. 'So am I.'

I thought it would be uncool to ask outright, 'Are you Allen Ginsberg?' Instead I asked him something which would be a ridiculous question if he was not who I thought he might be.

'Have you been doing any writing since you came to Scotland?'

'No not really,' he said, 'but I have lots of ideas. I'm taking notes. I hope to be inspired by Iona, such a special place I am told.'

Thus began my short friendship with Allen Ginsberg.

His travelling companion was a young Glaswegian lad he had met up with the night before. Ginsberg was gay and his poetry contains frequent allusions to his gregarious sexuality. I told him early on in our conversations that I was living with my partner Carolyn.

We started talking about the book I was reading. Ginsberg had not yet seen a copy in print and was curious to see what it said about him. We talked a lot about Kerouac, Ginsberg laughing as he recalled his failed attempts to persuade Kerouac into his bed.

Sometimes there's an instant affinity and you can converse with a new acquaintance as though you have known them forever. Ginsberg and I talked and talked, largely about eastern religions (Ginsberg was a Buddhist), and about politics, poetry (about which I knew very little), books, India, gurus, American life, New York – it continued like this for the next week. Some topics I shied away from. I would have loved to talk about his friendship with Dylan, but respecting Dylan's desire for privacy, it was a topic I largely avoided, feeling it to be intrusive.

Ginsberg and his friend were staying at Black's farm on Iona, and I was camping above the brilliant white sands of the north end of the island. Ginsberg was a little restricted in his movement, having recently broken his leg, but managed with some help to get about most of the island. We would meet up in the morning and make our way across to the Abbey area, or to the other side of the island, to the Bay at the back of the Ocean. Iona was at its best – blue sky, calm seas, the wild flowers on the machair a blaze of colour, skylarks singing – perfect summer weather. We talked a lot, stopping occasionally to sit quietly, absorbing the intense beauty of the island and its deep sense of peace and spirituality. One afternoon while we were sitting on the sand dunes, Ginsberg read out a poem he was working on and gave a recitation of 'Howl' to me, a few bemused sheep and the seagulls overhead.

Allen Ginsberg, was perhaps more keenly aware of the power of language than anyone else I have met. Each word was carefully considered, weighed-up mentally before it was spoken. This slow, thoughtful syle of speech was also spiced with great humour.

I had planned to leave Iona the day before him and we arranged to meet in the Abbey on my last evening The day's visitors had gone, and it was empty. Ginsberg had brought his finger cymbals. He sat cross-legged on the floor in front of the altar, where the Abbey's acoustics were at their best, chanting in his deep, sonorous voice. He alternated Tibetan Buddhist-style chants with the better-known Hare Krishna chant, and some Vedic verses he had learned in India. The haunting sound he created reverberated around the walls of the Abbey.

He came down to see me onto the ferry the next morning. My last memory of him was hearing his voice, long after he was out of sight, echoing down the sound of Mull, chanting the ancient Hindu mantra of peace; 'Om, shanti, shanti, shanti.'

That summer we exchanged some photos and postcards and some time later I discovered a poem with a reference to his time on Iona.

In 'Mind Breaths', written in 1973, Ginsberg is watching his breath and imagines it traversing the world

> across the Channel rough black-green waves, in London's Piccadilly
>> beercans roll on concrete neath Eros' silver breast, the *Sunday Times* lifts and settles on wet fountain steps—
> Over Iona Isle blue day and balmy Inner Hebrides breeze...

~

Political activity at Edinburgh University was a lot calmer in the early to mid-seventies than it had been in the late sixties. Gordon Brown, the first student rector and future Prime Minister, had graduated at the same time as me and had also embarked on a postgraduate degree. I sometimes encountered him in my local, The Meadow Bar on Buccleuch Street. I became aware of how serious his political ambitions were when he and his Labour Party colleague Robin Cook turned up at a party. When someone started to roll up a joint, the two aspiring MPs grabbed their jackets and were out of the door in an instant.

Gordon had the most beautiful girlfriend called Margarita, who seemed devoted to him. I was at his flat with a small group of friends one winter's afternoon, sitting round a fire drinking tea. Margarita excused herself from the group and said she was going to phone home. As she picked up the receiver, there was a lull in the conversation and it was impossible not to hear her talking.

'Can I speak to the Queen?' she asked. She then started to speak in a language I did not recognise. Gordon noticed my puzzled expression.

'Margarita is the Crown Princess of Romania,' he explained. 'Her parents are the exiled King and Queen.'

~

To fulfil my part of the bargain for doing the postgraduate in Social Work, I duly turned up for work at Craigentinny Castle, the council Social Work offices. Carolyn had disappeared off to Yugoslavia to be with Adrian, with whom she eventually settled down and had three children. Single again, I had rented out my spare rooms to other students. One of these was a Humanities student called Alan, who rarely went out or socialised, hence I was a little surprised to find him entertaining some friends one night at the flat. He invited me to join them and after they left I asked about the girlfriend of one of his friends, a primary school teacher originally from Darlington.

'Yes, Linda's lovely isn't she?'

I agreed.

Many years later, Linda Tennick was to change both of her names. When she became a devotee of Bhagwan Shree Rajneesh, he gave her the new first name of Kshema. Then Tennick changed to Cooper, when she became my wife.

CHAPTER SEVEN

Heading to the Himalayas

A good traveller has no fixed plans and is not intent on arriving
—Lao Tzu

By 1978 I had five years' experience as a social worker under my belt and was getting restless. Parts of the job I loved, others I hated. Evening visits to drunk aggressive clients in Edinburgh housing schemes were not enjoyable. It was clear to me that the social work intervention I was practising was only papering over cracks created by poverty, inequality and bad housing, political issues no amount of social work was going to eradicate. Dealing with the problems experienced generation after generation in the same families was frustrating, to say the least. I did, however, very much enjoy working as part of a team, and my colleagues were a pleasure to be associated with.

Many of those I trained with were specialising and moving up the ladder of promotion. Their commitment was something I could not share. I had my own flat, enjoyed a bachelor's life about town, had a steady income, a car and good friends. Life was pretty good. But the feeling of restlessness was acute.

The solution arrived in the mail one morning in the form of a letter informing me that I had a thousand pounds in my superannuation fund. I had no idea what this was. When I phoned to enquire, I was told it was the sum that had been deducted to go into my pension pot.

'It's yours when you retire,' I was told. 'Unless you leave early, in which case you can claim it all.'

'You mean to tell me that if I resign from my job now you will give me a thousand pounds and if I don't I will have to wait until I am sixty-five?' I asked.

'That's correct.'

I handed in my letter of resignation the next morning.

I was planning on using this unexpected windfall to travel overland to India and beyond, but first I wanted to see Dylan, on tour in England for the first time since 1969. I went to his concerts in Earls Court, staying with TM friends and met up with Tilly Mortimore from Somerset, who was living and teaching TM in London. Dylan was to be the headline act at an open-air concert in July at Blackbushe airstrip in Surrey and we arranged to go together in a months' time. Tilly drove us there in her red, open-top sports car. When we arrived we were both a little dismayed to see the huge numbers which had gathered for this self-styled picnic. With over two hundred thousand people, it was reputedly the biggest gathering of humanity the country had ever seen. We arrived in mid-afternoon, and slowly worked our way through the masses of bodies until we found ourselves close to the front, but to one side of the stage.

When one act left to be replaced by another, the surge of people getting to their feet created substantial pressure on the high, solid wood fencing at our side. With a loud crack, a whole section gave way and about thirty people fell through. Security guards rushed in, and having ascertained that no-one was hurt, proceeded to push everyone back into the main area and nail up the wall. Tilly and I had fallen over and someone on the inside helped us to our feet and started chatting. We found ourselves inside a large compound, with plenty of room to move about and a wonderful view of the stage. That freedom from the pressure of the huge crowd on the other side of the fence was very welcome.

The man who had helped us to our feet was Dave Cousins, lead singer of a popular band called The Strawbs. Looking over his shoulder, I could see lots of other celebrities from the music and film business. Record companies were handing out free food and champagne. Tilly and I had been sealed up inside the celebrity enclosure, and we wanted to stay.

But there was a problem. Almost everyone was wearing a security pass around their neck and there were a couple of security men checking that people's passes were visible. I kept a constant look-out for them, making sure I kept out of their way. Tilly looked like she belonged and I felt confident she would not be challenged.

I let my concentration lapse, and felt a tap on my shoulder.

'May I see your guest pass, please?' I was politely asked.

Inwardly I groaned, but I had a last line of defence. There were one or two famous and instantly recognisable people there, and their passes were not visible, nor were they being asked to show one.

I glared at the security guard and said,

'Do you mean to say you don't recognise me?' I stormed off, waiting for him to follow and say, 'Well actually, no. Show me your pass.'

But he didn't. Although he must have wondered who this person was, I was not asked again.

It was a struggle finding the car in the dark after the concert and it was not until dawn was breaking that we eventually got back to Tilly's Somerset home.

~

In early August 1978 I set off on a long overland journey, using public transport, with the intention of reaching Kathmandu in time for Christmas.

Ten years had passed since I was last in Istanbul. The itinerant hippies seemed to have morphed into tourists, although there were still plenty of young travellers about. I had crossed the continent on a 'Magic Bus', a London-based operation which offered cheap bus rides to Istanbul and places further east. My ticket stopped in that city; from there I was on my own. Before leaving Edinburgh, I had outlined my plans to Reshad Feild, an English Sufi Sheikh I had met at a series of lectures he was giving at the university. He began his life in the public eye as one of The Springfields, the backing group to a highly successful chanteuse of the seventies, Dusty Springfield, but his commitment to Sufism developed out of his fascination with the spiritual teachings of Gurdjieff and Ouspensky. His books about his experiences in Turkey with the Mevlevi order of Dervishes I found fascinating; they were the first I had read that illustrated the possibility of living a life of mystical spirituality in the West.

'Go and see Mustapha,' he told me. 'He is the head of the Mevlevi order of Dervishes. Tell him I sent you.'

I was intrigued, as this was the same man Feild had described in his books, and who had led him around Turkey in the most extraordinary series of adventures. He had a small bookshop in the book bazaar, in Sultanahmet, the old part of the city. However, all the bookshops looked the same – small and with every available square inch occupied by literature, and with no name or number to identify them. In one, there was a man at the back, clearly the shop owner, who was being treated with enormous respect by his clientele. This was the man I was seeking. I approached him, introduced myself and passed on Reshad Feild's messages. My Turkish was non-existent and his English not a lot better. We struggled to understand each other, but with help from others in the shop I gathered I was being invited to join his group of Sufis for a meeting that evening. He also talked about going on to Konya, the centre of the Mevlevi Dervish order in southern Turkey, and although tempted by these offers I declined. My journey was taking me further east and I did not want to get sidetracked.

'Welcome to Asia' read the sign on the old Galata Bridge, which moved underneath you as it floated on top of the Bosporus. There was a sense of difference, of change that was almost palpable. Although the oldest part of the city is in Europe, once in Asia the streets seemed noisier, bristling with humanity, the traffic more chaotic, and the men and women wearing more traditional clothes. Smells were different too, and not always for the better, with the odour from broken sewers competing with the sweeter smell of spices, coffee, fruit and flowers from market stalls.

I was on a local bus to Turkey's capital, Ankara, only stopping there long enough to get an onward ticket to Erzurum, some six hundred miles further east. On a route largely the same as that used by St Paul, Alexander, the Crusaders on their way to attack infidels, and the Islamic defenders of their faith heading west, there was plenty to dream about but little to look at. Ankara was not disappointing as I had been told to expect little. Erzurum was worse. Not only was the architecture drab and uninteresting but the people seemed hostile. It felt like a city with no soul. After an overnight stop in a cheap hostel recommended by Tony Wheeler in my travelling bible, *Across Asia on the Cheap,* I was on my way again. A different bus, a different driver, and mostly different passengers, although there were a few travellers like myself heading for India and Nepal, with whom I would cross paths over the next few weeks.

The quickest and cheapest way out of the city was by minibus, which seemed to drive around in circles with the driver shouting out of the window at any passing stranger, stopping to pick up yet another passenger. We left the city seriously overloaded, heading for Doğubeyazit ('Doggybiscuits' as it was called by fellow travellers), the last town before the Iranian border. The road from Istanbul had been long, hot and dry, the buses mobile deathtraps, with nothing of interest to justify staying around to explore. For a few extra lira the driver took me onto the border, where I joined the long line of people waiting to get into Iran.

~

'Why do you want to go to Iran?' the official at the Iranian Embassy in London had demanded at my interview for an entry visa four months previously.

'Because it's in the way of India.' I cheekily replied.

The official sighed, glared at me and walked away, reappearing some ten minutes later with the requisite paperwork. This fine-looking office in South Kensington was soon to be largely destroyed by the SAS when they stormed in to end a siege of the building organised by an Iranian Arab group.

Despite having the right visas, the border guards were not going to make my entry easy. They were disappointed to see that the cash I was carrying was in the form of traveller's cheques, and hence I was in no position to give them the baksheesh which would have eased my transition into the country. Eventually they got bored and moved on to another Westerner, and I walked a hundred yards to a waiting minibus, stopping only to negotiate with one of the many money changers to cash in a traveller's cheque at an exchange rate almost double what a bank would have given me. The minibus waited until it was overcrowded before taking me to Tabriz, an industrialised city which, like Ankara and Erzurum, held no interest for me. Under different circumstances I would have liked to have seen some of the southern part of the land, Esfahan in particular, but Iran was a country in turmoil, not a place to tarry, and after a sleepless night in a noisy, grubby hotel, I was on the road again.

In Tehran I looked up the brother of a friend, who later described me as having that road-weary look of a man who has travelled too far, too fast. He and his partner were, like many other native English speakers in the country, earning substantial sums teaching English in local schools, universities and industrial complexes. They kindly invited me round for a meal, Jacob picking me up on his motorbike and taking me to their suburban flat. Most of their possessions were packed away in boxes littering the apartment floor.

'We have to be ready to leave at a moment's notice,' they explained. 'The situation here is very volatile, it's a bit like living on the rim of a volcano that's about to erupt.'

Mohammad Reza Shah Pahlavi, 'King of Kings', 'Light of the Aryans', but perhaps best-known as the Shah of Iran, ruled the land with an iron fist. He had progressive pro-Western policies and introduced a series of social, political and economic reforms thus modernising the nation and turning Iran into a global power. In his one-party state, any opposition was treated as treason. He was the first regional leader to recognise the State of Israel and he made strong allies with Europe and America. His enemies saw him as a puppet of Western powers, a dictator dependent on brutality, corruption and oppression, who had an extensive and vicious secret police force.

The previous October had seen the first demonstrations against the Shah. Strikes and bigger demonstrations followed. Exiled dissidents, including the Ayatollah Khomeini, were orchestrating a revolution. Violent change was imminent. My hosts were concerned about getting the money they had earned out of the country and planned to be back in the UK before the end of the year. We also had a curfew to worry about. Anyone seen outside after ten p.m. was likely to be shot. As we sped through the empty streets on Jacob's motorbike, we came to a deserted square, at the far end of which a tank was sitting, engine running. The barrel swivelled round in our direction and followed us as we crossed the square. Jacob made it safely back home that night and they both left the country immediately after the next major demonstration in September when government troops opened fire on the crowd, killing dozens. That spelled the end of the road for the Shah, who exiled himself to Egypt early in the New Year, after which Iran closed its borders to the West.

Although he was a Muslim, the Shah's downfall was in large part due to his attempts to drag Iran into a future as a secular state. His programme of modernisation included the education of women, who were also given the right to vote and the relaxation of the strict dress code that more fundamentalist Islamic countries imposed. Hostile clergy exerted significant control over the opinions of the mass of the population. I am no politician, but I cannot understand why successive Western governments dealing with Iran, and indeed its neighbour to the east, repeatedly try to apply political or military solutions to crises which are embedded in religious traditions. Any attempt to seek a positive outcome which ignores the religious element seems doomed to failure.

My accommodation hardly merited the title of a hotel, but that is how it was listed in my guidebook. It certainly provided cheap accommodation, and the owner was helpful and spoke good English. Occasionally there was hot water but most of the time there was no water at all. The toilet was the Asian-style elevated pedestal above a hole in the tiles, which after a day or two without water was disgusting. Rooms were not cleaned from one occupant to the next, and the single sheet probably hadn't been washed for weeks. Fortunately, I had a sheet sleeping bag with me for occasions such as these. The only livestock I knowingly shared the room with was a large gecko. I had never seen one before, but was reassured that not only was it harmless, but that it was adept at eating up mosquitoes and other unwanted bugs in the room.

I had a couple of days in the city before I was able to start travelling again, and there were a couple of things I needed to do. Driven by curiosity and unfounded faith that I would come to no harm, I ignored advice to stay clear of the bazaar area where, so I was told, even the police would not go. When I bought some fruit from a market stall, I was careful to do as I had been instructed and hand over a note with the image of the Shah face down. Nevertheless the stallholder turned the note over to spit on the picture of the Shah's face before putting the money away.

On my way to the central post office to collect any poste restante mail, I stumbled across a carpet-makers' area; streets laid out with rugs of all shapes and sizes, some huge, some with the most complex and intricate patterns, others richly-coloured works of woven art. The traffic was driving over them as if they were not there. These carpets were being worn into the cobbles by horse drawn carts, taxis, even the occasional tank. 'Old rugs fetch more money,' a weaver explained. 'This way a new carpet can be made to look old in a week!'

At the post office there was a letter from Tony and Ursula. Their seasonal business was now closed and they had decided to head out to India themselves, rightly feeling that they could cope with the overland journey using public transport, despite being in their late sixties. They wrote to say that by the time I read this, they would be on their way. I sent them a card to the Istanbul Post Office, advising them to hasten through Iran and that I would look for them at the Kathmandu Guest House on Christmas Eve.

My journey continued up past the southern shore of the

Caspian Sea, then followed a route just south of the Russian border, stopping in Mashhad, the second holiest city to Islam after Mecca and a place at the best of times antipathetic to foreigners, but in the current political climate potentially dangerous.

Leaving Iran was relatively straightforward. The Afghanistan border was little more than a few semi-derelict sheds in the desert. The queue of cars, taxis, buses and minibuses stretched back as far as the eye could see. The vehicles were given a perfunctory search by bored-looking young soldiers in army fatigues and trainers. In an office with cracked glass windows sat a man, rifle by his side, stamping passports. Another wanted to see evidence of money being brought in to the country, a third checked visas. Whilst all this was going on, a steady stream of humanity, bent double under loads fixed by a rope around their foreheads, staggered along in the intense noonday heat past the soldiers, who completely ignored them. Were these refugees escaping from the threat of an imminent regime change in Iran? Shiites or Sunnis fleeing possible retribution? Or were they simply traders who did this journey regularly? Whatever the case, it made a mockery of the border controls I had just experienced.

There was an element of jumping from the frying pan into the fire going from Iran to Afghanistan, which had for centuries been subjected to attempted invasions from different colonial powers. As the buffer between Russia and British India, in the late nineteenth-century the country became the theatre for 'The Great Game', when stories of spies, dangerous expeditions, bizarre behaviour by eccentric explorers were rife.

Six months before I crossed the border, the Communist Party had seized control of Afghanistan, which triggered civil war in the mountainous north. These mujahidin, regarded as freedom fighters by the West and funded and armed with weapons which would be used against their benefactors in future years. In the seventies the Americans and the Russians had been currying favour with neutral Afghanistan, building roads, hospitals, schools, airports and other vital infrastructure. In 1978 the Russians were in evidence acting as advisers in the battle against the mujahidin, but their disastrous military invasion was still several months away. For me it seemed as if everywhere I went was in political upheaval and I feared for the safety of Tony and Ursula who were by now about a thousand miles west of me.

But I was really enjoying the country. The Afghans I met were impressive people, the full-bearded men tall, polite and helpful, but most of all, proud. Their culture was one of welcoming strangers into their midst, but with a degree of pity for anyone who had the misfortune of being born elsewhere. I spent a few days in Herat, an old city full of character with ancient walls, fertile gardens and bustling street markets. War was soon to reduce this historic place to rubble, as indeed Kandahar, my next stopping place. People had been living here for the last seven thousand years and had seen many invasions, destruction and rebuilding. I could almost feel the spirit of Alexander the Great, Genghis Khan, Tamerlane and others who came to conquer and reign in this geographically strategic city. The only difference now was that the weapons were more sophisticated. Each time the city was destroyed it was rebuilt by its new occupier and the same continues today, as buildings razed by cruise missiles fired against the Taliban are restored or replaced.

Like Istanbul, Kabul was a hippie bottleneck. I caught up with many of the people I had seen over meals in Chicken Street cafés. They all had their own stories to tell, mostly involving army, police or local wildlife. Steve, a tall man with a body like string, recounted how he had been stung on the ankle by a scorpion in Herat. He killed it with his sandal, and with the insect's body in a paper bag, hobbled painfully to the local hospital. The doctors and nurses crowded around him, laughing and pointing first at Steve's swelling ankle, then at the dead scorpion, before wandering off, leaving Steve to deal with the pain on his own.

My own brush with authority had a positive, unexpected outcome.

'What kind of revolution are you trying to make in this country?' I perhaps foolishly demanded of the Russian General, who towered above my six foot, two inch frame. But I was seriously hacked off and as he was standing at the ticket office, he was the nearest target to vent my anger on. I had turned up at the main Kabul stadium to spend a day at the national Buzkashi championships, a week-long event which involved two teams of horsemen and a decapitated goat. Fifty dollars, way above my budget, was the designated rate for foreigners, whereas locals were allowed in for the equivalent of a few pennies.

The general was impassive. I was not even sure he understood English, so I continued, hoping he did not.

'You are charging an outrageous price! Just because someone comes from the West does not mean they are rich. I am an Anthropology student, and would love to witness what is going on here but you make this impossible. What do you want me to report back to my friends and colleagues when I get home? That Russia is a capitalist, exploitative state only interested in how much money it can make from people?'

The general burst out laughing.

'Come and see me tomorrow, my friend,' he replied in perfect, but heavily accented English. 'I will see what I can do.'

The game of Buzkashi, dating back to the thirteenth century, evolved in Afghanistan and neighbouring Pakistan from tribal regions where warring clans would raid each other's villages on horseback at full gallop, leaning out of the saddle to grab whatever they could as they flew past. Women, livestock, anything of value was taken. Perhaps as a practice session for such raids, horsemen would train by picking up a dead goat as they galloped by. Possibly as inter-tribal treaties were formed, the fighting skills were adapted for sport. Seven centuries later the game was the national sport of Afghanistan, with both teams and some individual players having cult status. The national championships in Kabul drew massive crowds into the stadium for the daily knockout rounds.

I duly arrived the following afternoon, and my general friend was standing in the same place as before. 'Mr Cooper,' he called, and led me away from the crowd at the gate. We went through a side entrance, along dark corridors, up a flight of stairs, and back outside, where the light from the noon sun momentarily blinded me. I realised I was in the equivalent of a Royal or VIP box at Twickenham or Murrayfield, with a fine view of the arena and the company of about a dozen other suited individuals I suspected to be politicians and a few Russian officers. I was introduced to some, but was able to converse with none. The general said I was his guest for the afternoon, showed me to my seat and returned to his duties at the entrance. I did not see him again.

The 'ball' was led onto the field. On this occasion it was a large goat, but a calf was also acceptable, and would be used as the championships reached the closing stages at the end of the week. There was a new 'ball' for each game. A sword flashed in the bright sun as the goat was decapitated. Within a few seconds the hooves were cut off, the poor beast was gutted and the game was ready to start.

The goat's body was collected by a man on horseback, apparently a referee of sorts. He dropped the body at one end of the field, blew a whistle, and subsequently took little part in proceedings. The game seemed anarchic. At the sound of the whistle the two teams of about twenty riders gathered at the far ends of the stadium, then charged at full gallop down the turf, stopping at the goat. Someone would lean far out of the saddle and try to pick up the dead beast. Imagine a rugby maul, but instead of a dozen men scrabbling for the ball, there were forty horses with their riders all fighting to grab the goat and no rules as to what was unacceptable behaviour. With horses trained to stand still when their rider was leaning out of the saddle, others would grab its reins to get it to move, or use a stick on its flanks or on the hands of the rider trying to grab the goat. Horses would rear up, their hooves flailing in the air, often making contact with another rider or horse. A cacophony of sound reverberated about the field. Horses snorting and neighing, hooves thumping the ground, men shouting, the crowd cheering, a constant commentary coming over the tannoy. Dust from the parched earth soon covered animals, riders and those in the front rows of the audience. Occasionally a rider would break free from the pack with the goat in hand, the others in hot pursuit. To huge acclaim from the crowd, he would drop the goat in a circle marked out by paint, making a score for his side. The goat was then taken back to one end of the field, and at the blow of a whistle the whole astonishing spectacle would start over again.

This mayhem continued for two hours. It stopped twice in that time, the first time to answer the call to prayer from a nearby minaret, when the entire audience and players, with the exception of the non-Muslims in my enclosure, turned to Mecca and, like a murmuration of starlings coming into roost, moved as a single body, kneeling, standing, prostrating, and praying. The second time was when two riders broke free from the melee, one carrying the goat's front feet, the other the rear. Neither was inclined to let go. Their horses charged to the far end of the stadium, in unison cleared a fence and raced through the gap the parting crowd created, out onto the traffic-filled street. After about five minutes one rider reappeared, goat in hand.

I have never experienced anything quite like this chaotic, dangerous, bloody event so beloved by the Afghans. What I was not to know then, of course, was what was going to happen in this same stadium in future years. When the mujahedeen eventually came to power, this was the venue for much more gruesome events; public limb amputations for thieves, death by stoning for adulterers and homosexuals, hangings or beheadings for those who in any way opposed the ruling regime.

I was keen to see more of the country. First, however, I needed some cash, and was curious about the numerous black-market money-changers, often young lads, who seemed to occupy every street corner.

Although the banks offered an official exchange rate, it was possible to get a better deal changing money on the black market. The lads were on a commission basis for one or two major dealers in the free market exchange. I approached one I had seen every day on Chicken Street. He called me 'Scottie' after I told him where I came from. He could not have been any older than twelve, and though obviously not attending school, he was gaining an education on this busy Kabul street. As well as his native tongue, he was able to converse in English, German, Dutch, French, Italian and a smattering of Nordic languages. He worked the street with an intelligence which shone. But it was his ability with figures, combined with an extraordinary memory for current exchange rates, which was astounding.

'I want to change some money,' I said to Rashid, sitting down beside him on the empty orange box he provided for his customers.

'No problem, Scottie, no problem.' He was one of those people for whom anything was 'no problem'. 'What currencies?'

'Dollars and sterling traveller's cheques.'

'And you want to buy?'

'What have you got?'

He proceeded to reel off the major currencies of Asia, and with each an exchange rate far in excess of the official one. In particular what he was offering for the Afghani was almost double what I would get across the street in the bank. I was reluctant to change much as I did not want to be carrying cash, but bought currency for India and Pakistan and enough for the rest of my stay in Afghanistan.

'You going to Nepal?' he asked, 'I have a special rate for you.'

And he did. However I felt insecure about parting with more traveller's cheques.

'You cash a cheque?' I asked.

His reply was predictable. 'No problem.'

I proceeded to write out a cheque for fifty pounds, leaving the payee blank. He disappeared for a couple of minutes, reappearing with a smile and a fistful of currencies, counting each out into my hand, ensuring I was happy that the rate offered was the rate paid.

I hope he survived the turmoil his country was rushing towards.

When I eventually returned home, there was an envelope of bank statements and cashed cheques waiting for me. Amongst them was the cheque I had given to this lad on a Kabul street. It had been through many hands. Grubby and worn, the payee scored out and changed, with different initials and scribblings in foreign script on the back, it had found its way back to my bank in Edinburgh and had been honoured.

The old Silk Road was what connected the markets of China with the Western world, and it was along this I headed next, up into the Hindu Kush to the fertile Bamiyan valley. On their way through, the Chinese had brought Buddhism with them and monks had settled in the area in the second century, creating monasteries and monk's cells in the soft sandstone cliffs which dominated the valley. Here Buddhism thrived for five hundred years. In the last half of the sixth century the monks carved two enormous statues of Buddha into the rock, the largest some fifty-three metres tall, the tallest standing statues of Buddha in the world.

With no trappings of modern tourism, no signs to the statues and hardly a path to reach them, when you turned a corner there they were, towering above you. It took your breath away. The exquisitely detailed brightly-coloured frescoes at the side of the statues were in excellent condition, despite there having been no maintenance work carried out on the site over the centuries. With a little exploration you could climb stairs hewn out of the rock surrounding the statues and come out just above the top of the head, looking out to the valley stretching out below. Sadly, an Afghan king partly destroyed the faces in the 1880s. Perhaps that was a portent as to their eventual fate. Despite it being a UNESCO World Heritage site, in March 2001 the Taliban starting using heavy artillery to blast these beautiful monuments to bits. What had taken a generation to build, had lasted fifteen hundred years, was reduced to rubble in just three months.

CHAPTER EIGHT

In the Land of the Great Game

The Khyber Pass had been a place of my fantasies and dreams. As a child, I had enjoyed Rudyard Kipling's adventures of derring-do based in this area and latterly the stories of the Great Game – the name Kipling gave to that shadowy struggle between Victorian Britain and Tsarist Russia over the early exploration of the Hindu Kush, Northern Pakistan, Northern India, Kashmir, Baltistan and Tibet – had kept me enthralled into the small hours of many a night. As the ancient bus rattled higher into the pass, my thoughts turned to some of those intrepid explorers who had passed this way not with conquering armies, but on foot or horseback, sometimes alone, sometimes with a small entourage, but all with extraordinary drive, courage or foolhardiness and often an abundance of luck.

Some were travellers, some geographers, some were soldiers, some spies, some were eccentric, and all perhaps were a combination of these. Travelling at a time when there were no roads or maps, poorly equipped in mountainous terrain occupied by hostile tribal people who would have no hesitation to kill strangers especially if they were infidels. To avoid capture and to allay suspicion as to his true identity, Joseph Wolfe travelled several hundred miles deep into the Western Himalaya. Posing as a mad dervish, he went everywhere stark naked. It was easier to identify with John Wood, if only because we shared a childhood in Perthshire and Argyll. Suffering frostbite, he struggled over mountain passes and frozen rivers to discover the source of the river Oxus. Another Scot, a first cousin of our national bard, was Alexander Burnes who surveyed the river Indus and crossed the Hindu Kush into Uzbekistan. He shared his cousin's liking for the ladies and his murder in Kabul, at the hands of the husbands whose wives he had slept with, sparked off the First Afghan War. This was the worst defeat suffered by the British Army in Asia, not surpassed until the fall of Singapore in 1941. Alexander Gardner, another adventurer with Scottish roots, was possibly the first Westerner to get into Kafiristan, somewhere I had hopes of reaching. He chose as the epigraph for his autobiography, a poem from Robert Louis Stevenson's *Songs of Travel*: '...My mistress still the open road, and the bright eyes of danger.'

In the 1890s George Scott Robertson left his remote Orkney homeland for the even more remote Nuristan, eventually living for a year amongst the Kafir Kalash. He survived and was the first to write a book about these enigmatic mountain people.

Andrew Dalgleish was a Scottish merchant, traveller, government spy, and the first from the West to start trading in Ladakh. In 1888 he was hacked to death by an Afghan in a lonely pass in the Karakoram. Three times George Hayward crossed the Western Himalaya with no supplies and in the dead of winter, for which he received the highest accolades from the Royal Geographical Society. After a short military career in the Cameron Highlanders he had sold his commission and become an explorer. He too was murdered, beheaded as he left his tent. I did not know it then, but I was soon to stumble across his grave in Gilgit.

The second Westerner to reach Skardu was a wild Scottish adventurer and doctor named John Henderson, who in 1835, wearing only tattered native dress, followed the Indus down from Leh and then crossed south to Srinagar.

In 1847 another Scot, Thomas Thomson, a botanist working with the Boundary Commission demarcating the borders of Kashmir, travelled from Ladakh to Skardu, where he spent the winter before crossing the Zoji La Pass to Srinagar. He took many plants back to England with him and ended his days happily in Kew Gardens in London, recognised as one of the greatest botanists of his time.

Then there was William MacNair, who, disguised as a Muslim doctor was the first Westerner to cross the Lowari Pass into Chitral in 1883, going on across the Shandur Pass to Gilgit and Srinagar. Some of these leading players in the Great Game were recruited and trained by Sir Charles Metcalfe MacGregor, Quarter Master General of the Indian Army, and founder of the Indian Army's Intelligence Department. He claimed his descendancy from Rob Roy MacGregor. Colonel William Lockhart, son of a Scottish minister, became the first Commander in Chief in India and established the first British Army presence in Chitral. Perhaps the greatest was the eccentric William Moorcroft who travelled extensively in Northern India, Northern Pakistan and Tibet. He died of a fever in Afghanistan not far from where I was sitting in the bus now. The presence and influence of these extraordinary men was to be felt for decades, haunting the land from Tibet to the Caspian Sea. Few died peacefully, even fewer made it back to their mother country.

My reverie was broken by the sound of wheels crunching on gravel as the bus came to a halt high in the mountains in the middle of the Khyber Pass. The door opened and two men entered, looking like they had just walked off of a film set. Bearded and weather-beaten, scarves wrapped around their heads, wearing boots and baggy trousers, with bandoliers crossing their chests and old Lee Enfield .303 rifles over their shoulder, they might as well have had 'bandit' written across their foreheads. And although that is exactly what they were, they seemed quite benign, sharing a joke with the driver and giving only a cursory glance at the occupants of the bus. They were hill tribesmen, Taliban in infancy, who were stopping every vehicle using the pass and extracting a 'toll' to allow them to proceed. The driver was prepared for this and handed over the little extra money he had asked his passengers for when he had sold us our tickets. With a shout and a wave they were off and we were on our way again.

It seemed like there was nothing in the world which you could not buy in the street markets of Peshawar, in particular if arms were your interest. Stalls stretched in all directions with every conceivable type of weapon on display. I was looking for something to fight a stomach bug, and the man running the hotel I was staying at had sent me into the bazaar to look for the local opium dealer. Sure enough he was where I had been told to find him, sitting cross-legged on his street stall underneath a sign which read 'Opium' in English. When I told him of my messy symptoms he pulled out a packet from a drawer by his side and extracted a large block of a black sticky substance. He pulled off a very small amount which he rolled into a ball in his fingers.

'Take this, my friend,' he said. 'It is raw opium. You will sleep well, you will have no side effects, it will cure your stomach bug.' I followed his instructions and woke up after eight hours of deep sleep, feeling fine.

I was keen to get back into the mountains, and now that I was feeling better, took a minibus north to Chitral less than two hundred miles away. I knew it was going to be a long, uncomfortable trip. After forty miles we left the fertile plains and started climbing. The road deteriorated. Soon it was a narrow dirt track that twisted and turned through innumerable hairpin bends. Fortunately the worst of the journey, where the road dropped away vertiginously into a raging torrent of a river below, was at night, and the drop a few inches from the wheels was sensed but not seen. The driver told me he preferred to drive in the dark unable to see the rusting vehicles wrecked at the bottom of the cliffs.

I arrived in Chitral tired and ready for breakfast.

It was like a frontier town. The unsurfaced streets separated old wood and mortar buildings with a boardwalk for a pavement, along which tradesman plied their craft. Young boys ran up and down noisily playing hoop-la with a stick and the rim of a rusty old bicycle wheel. I needed a haircut, and sat on a chair on the pavement, whilst the barber snipped away. On my right a dentist was drilling some poor local man's tooth with a drill driven from a foot pedal, chatting to passers-by in the process. On my left an educated English-speaking local man was having his morning shave with an open razor. When the barber's cloak was removed it revealed an army uniform.

'I am the local District Officer,' he proudly introduced himself. His indeed was a position of some power. The arrival of a British traveller was of interest to him, because he wanted to speak and be seen speaking English to this stranger. He was friendly and keen to help.

'I would like to get into Kafiristan, to visit the valleys of the Kafir Kalash people,' I told him one morning over a cup of tea in a chai house. Pleased that I was showing an interest in local culture, he promised to give me the necessary permits which would allow me into the area.

'The Wearers of the Black Robes' are an intriguing people. Numbering just a few thousand, they live in three isolated valleys north-west of Chitral. Their ancestry is unclear, but accepted wisdom has it that they are the descendants of some of the soldiers of Alexander the Great who passed by this way, though the evidence to support the claim is controversial. They are light-skinned, blue-eyed and non-Muslim, practising a mixture of ancestor worship and animism. Their isolation has protected their beliefs, ideology and way of living. To their credit, the Government of Pakistan has passed legislation making it an imprisonable offence for any representative of any religion to try and convert these people.

Of the three valleys they occupied I was heading for the largest, Brumburet. I got a short lift to where the road ended, then embarked on a twenty-five mile hike up into the Hindu Kush foothills on a well-worn footpath, which crossed and recrossed the same river innumerable times. The bridges were round logs with no handrail, close enough to the water to be wet and slippery. I had a heavy backpack and the first was crossed slowly and with great caution, but several hours later I was treating the hazards like a seasoned local.

This was a glorious hike in perfect weather. I walked, climbing slowly all day. By late afternoon I came across a man fixing a break in an intricate irrigation system which I had been following for the last mile or two. The Kafir Kalash have their own language of which I did not know a word, but his smile was welcoming and it was clear he could use some help shifting stones onto the wall of the water channel. We worked in silence for a short while, then, job done, he led me a little further up the valley to the settlement of houses perched about a half mile up from the river on the south-facing slopes of the mountains. There was no accommodation dedicated for visitors in the valley, but he took me to a building which a Dutch couple were using as their base. They were a husband and wife team, an anthropologist and a linguist, who had been living there for the past five months gathering data for their respective PhDs. This was to be my home for the next week.

I was fortunate to have the company of Leo and Astrid, who were able to tell me more about the area and its inhabitants. The black robes and long ornate cowrie-shell headdresses were not for ceremonial occasions, but for everyday use. The cowrie shells they could still find locally, evidence of the time when this area, now so far from the sea, was coastal. In contrast with the rest of the country, the sexes were encouraged to mix. Women not only had the freedom to choose their own partner, but could change husbands by writing to the prospective new one, saying how much her current husband had paid for her and telling him she was his if he paid double. Perhaps four goats instead of two. Marriage by elopement was not unusual and carried no stigma. This would happen at festival time, of which those of autumn, winter and spring were the most important. These occasions involved a lot of music and dancing, goats were slaughtered and homemade wine drunk. I found the people hospitable and fun to be around, but after a week it was time to move on.

Although well into November and an autumnal feeling still in the air, winter was not far off. My plan was to get to Gilgit, which meant heading south again for a couple hundred miles, before I could pick up a road north-west for a few hundred more miles. I did not relish the thought of using public transport on these roads for such distances, but there was an alternative. Gilgit was roughly on the same parallel as Chitral. There were roads directly connecting the towns, which are about three hundred miles apart. The problem was that in the middle of this route was the Shandur Pass, which would now be closed for winter. But not to foot traffic.

Back in Chitral, I broached the subject with the District Officer. I would need his authorisation to be wandering about in what was still a politically sensitive area. He radioed around his colleagues and was told that although the pass was covered in snow it was still negotiable by foot. The forecast for the next few days was good.

Thea Sigmund, a Dutch woman with high altitude walking experience, wanted to join me. So did an Italian man called Carlo whose English was not good. He maintained he had good boots and warm clothes and was fit for the trip. I was not convinced but it was not my call to say no. They obtained the necessary paperwork and just before dawn the following morning we picked up a jeep going to Mastuj, the last settlement before we would start walking. The District Officer had arranged for us to stay with a friend of his, a tribal leader who lived in the highest house in the village. The headman fed us and kindly, given the lack of trees in the area, provided a fire in the room we slept in. He appeared very early in the morning with a visitors' book to sign. The last name, entered over two years previously, was that of my anthropology tutor at Edinburgh University.

It was another dawn start. We had a long day in front of us, and no idea how severe conditions might be. The track was just discernible in the morning gloom. I knew it was about fifteen miles to the top of the pass, not so certain how far to the first settlement on the other side, but did know that we had to reach it. We all had our own sleeping bags but no tent and not a lot of food. Our spirits rose with the sun, and we kept a good pace.

Feeling a little responsible for the group and not knowing what lay ahead I discouraged stops to appreciate the staggeringly beautiful scenery. It became apparent that Thea was going to be fine, but Carlo was moving slower than us and seemed to be struggling with his backpack.

'What have you got in here?' I asked him. We had stopped for a short break and I had lifted his discarded pack to feel the weight. It was very heavy.

His English was not good and I was not sure he understood. I tried again.

'You are carrying too much.' I said pointing to his bag. 'Are you sure you need it all?'

Carlo opened his backpack, removed a layer of clothes, then a large oilskin package which he proceeded to unwrap. To my horror its contents were revealed as twelve large, probably kilo blocks of cannabis. No wonder he wanted to find an obscure way across the country and why he could not take a flight out. The reality of the situation hit home. We were going to be passing police checkpoints. The three of us could find ourselves in serious trouble.

Soon after setting off again we were overtaken by a group of Pakistani locals. One introduced himself by standing to attention, giving a formal military salute and stating his name, rank and serial number. He was ex-British Army and proud of it. His English was good and he was offering us his services to act as a guide over the mountain. He and his two companions were making the last crossing of the pass that winter back to their homes in the Gilgit District. Although the route was obvious and we were unlikely to get lost, we readily accepted his offer. We were now a party of six.

We were soon above the snow line, climbing steadily. Fortunately the snow was crisp and crunchy, and we did not have to force our way through it. The day was glorious, blue skies and a few puffy white clouds, no sign at all that this was going to change in the next few hours. The beauty of this pristine mountain wilderness was sublime.

Towards the bealach, the summit of the pass, Carlo was really struggling. It was cold, and at fourteen thousand feet the effects of altitude were kicking in. Despite his protestations at the outset that he had adequate gear, it turned out that he had no decent boots or jacket. One of the three locals took his backpack and added that to his own load, which allowed Carlo to keep up with the rest us.

I had anticipated that the descent would be straightforward but I had not accounted for the route being more exposed on its eastern flank. Snow had been blown into thick drifts across our path. We took it in turns to break the trail.

A little more than eighty years earlier Colonel James Kelly had come this way, heading west in a desperate attempt to relieve the siege of Chitral, where the British and Sikh troops had been under attack in their Chitral citadel for weeks. Severely outnumbered and running low on food and ammunition, they were facing certain, imminent and unpleasant death. Kelly had left Gilgit with two large pieces of heavy artillery, four hundred Sikh pioneers, forty Kashmiri Sappers and a hundred irregular soldiers drafted in from Hunza. It was early March and the Shandur Pass was seemingly impassable. Kelly forced the march, and in a brilliant piece of military leadership, used one group to break the trail, another to take the big guns apart, put the pieces on sledges and drag them along, and another to round up the support group who had bolted with the food and the ponies. To speed up the journey they had no tents and slept out in the open. Suffering from frostbite, snow blindness, soaked to the skin, often sinking to their armpits in the snow, they hauled themselves and their equipment up and over the pass. It took three days to get ten miles, a remarkable feat with no loss of life and just fifty-five cases of frostbite. The siege of Chitral was broken by the extraordinary bravery and perseverance of Kelly and his men.

We made it to Laspur, a tiny settlement, by late afternoon. One of our guides arranged accommodation and food in a single-room, stone-walled building, which we shared with the family and their goats. The fire was in the centre of the room and the smoke barely escaped from the small hole in the roof, making for an uncomfortable night. The next morning, red-eyed and with sore lungs, we walked on to the next village where we arranged a lift to Gilgit.

I do not think I am ghoulish or have a preoccupation with death, but I do find graveyards fascinating, especially in remote foreign locations. You can get a feel for the social history of the place, particularly where the surrounding area has been of military or geographical interest. Gilgit's graveyards are divided by ethnicity and religion. The Chinese has the graves of hundreds of workers killed in the construction of the Karakoram Highway. The European graveyard is filled with graves of soldiers and their families, a few climbers and one of the greatest explorers of them all, George Hayward.

I had a quiet few days in the town, watched a couple of polo matches, walked in the surrounding countryside, drank lots of tea and talked to the small group of travellers whose paths had merged in Gilgit. I had originally contemplated moving further east to Skardu in the heart of the Karakoram, but the only road in was now shut off for the winter. Although flights were cheap, they were unreliable and infrequent, and probably beyond my budget.

However I had not anticipated that the Hunza valley would be open again. For the past twenty years the Chinese had been building the Karakoram highway in an area where the engineering problems were as significant as the political. At the confluence of the Karakoram, Hindu Kush and Himalaya mountain ranges and passing close to the borders of Afghanistan, Pakistan, and China, the project was sensitive strategically and militarily, hence the entire section north of Gilgit was off limits. Thousands of Pakistani and Chinese labourers had been killed in the construction, mostly by landslide, in one case wiping out an entire construction camp. The Chinese in particular were keen to keep statistics like this under wraps. But this had changed, and the day I arrived in Gilgit, the highway was opened up to Hunza. This was an opportunity not to miss. Thea was keen to go as well, and after making a few enquiries, found a jeep which would take us. We were to be the first Westerners into Hunza for a decade.

It is little more than fifty miles from Gilgit to Hunza, but before the new road this was a seven-hour jeep journey, with an accumulated rise and fall of over fifty thousand feet. The new highway made this a short and pleasant drive. We headed for Baltit, the biggest village in the valley, and the only place foreigners could stay. At the far end there was a manned barrier with a large new sign forbidding any further progress. Although part of Pakistan, the valley was effectively controlled by the Mir of Hunza, a hereditary position whose control of the area was almost absolute. He was the judge and jury of any conflict over property. His decisions were respected and adhered to. He occupied the largest and highest building in the area, Baltit Fort, from the flat roof of which he could survey his domain.

I spent my days walking, exploring and talking to locals. Because of the historic influence of the British Army in the area, it was surprising how many people could speak a little English. The local schoolteacher spent time with me showing me around and introducing me to others. We were something of a curiosity, especially with the children, for whom we were the first Westerners they had seen. I was asked to talk to the kids in the classroom, with the teacher translating.

Hunza has the reputation for being one of the healthiest environments in the world. With almost complete dependence on locally produced food, no imports of any processed junk food or drink, no sugar, abstinence from alcohol, no use of fertilisers, and the unpolluted air of high altitude living, it was not hard to see why. Longevity was the norm. I met several fit-looking men still working the fields who maintained that they were centenarians, but with the lack of birth records that would have been difficult to prove. They also had acres of apricot trees, and after eating the fruit they would eat the kernel in the middle of the stone, which supposedly contains anti-cancer properties.

Although I imagine the winter months could be cold, dark and miserable, there were enough vestiges of autumn to make this look like a special place. The poplar trees lined the fields, pointing up towards the enormous mountains which dominated the view, in particular Rakaposhi, which at twenty-five thousand feet is only the twenty-seventh highest mountain in the world; if you take its uninterrupted vertical height of six thousand metres, it's the tallest mountain there is. The acres of apricot orchards would be a wonderful sight when in blossom, but I enjoyed walking through them devoid of flowers and leaves, out along some of the original mountain track used before the first road into the valley was built. Not for long, however. The narrowing path on the sheer rock-face and huge drops below soon became outwith my comfort zone and I scurried back.

Word had reached the ears of the Mir of Hunza that young travellers had arrived in Baltit. There were five of us by this time and we all received an invitation to take tea in the Baltit Fort with the Mir. We were shown around, and then sat in a circle on some deep red, intricately patterned carpets whilst the Mir, who had completed his education in England, asked us individually where we came from.

'Scotland,' I said when it was my turn.

'Ah, Scotland,' he said. 'I know someone from Scotland. He was a climber, on an expedition to climb Rakaposhi. My wife knitted him a jumper. Now what was his name?' He thought for a moment. 'Hamish!' he said. 'That's right, Hamish MacInnes.'

The world suddenly felt very small. Hamish is my near neighbour in Glencoe. In his day he was one of the world's top mountaineers.

Back in Hunza the weather was changing and I did not relish the thought of being stuck in northern Pakistan for the winter. It was time to head south. In Gilgit I treated myself to the luxury of a flight to Rawalpindi. Local flights were heavily subsidised, costing only a little more than the bus, but infinitely more comfortable.

There were only three flights a week on a little thirty-seater

Fokker Friendship. The first available was in a couple of days' time. I duly arrived at the airport, which was little more than a shed at the edge of a large field. The flying sock was the only indication that planes might land and take off from here. I had a valid ticket for the flight out, but the previous two flights earlier in the week had been cancelled due to bad weather over the mountains, and there were effectively three plane-loads of people, all believing that their claim to a seat on the next flight was valid. Chaos reigned, with much pushing and shoving, arguing and shouting, until the staff at the check-in gave up and walked away. The incoming flight landed, and the disembarking passengers were met by a horde of people, myself included, rushing across the field, scrambling for a seat on the plane. Being quite fit I reached the aircraft before all the seats were taken. The hostess approached asking if I would give up my seat as there was such a demand for space – the Captain had seen me running for the plane, and was offering me the spare seat in the cockpit! Right after take-off we did a flypast of the twenty-six thousand feet Nanga Parbat, skirting around the snow, rock and ice of the impressive north face. Flying over the Himalayas in perfect conditions with a one hundred and eighty degree view from the cockpit, it remains the best flight I have ever been on.

Islamabad is connected to the vast Indian railway network and although buying a ticket east was simple, getting on the train was more problematic. The platform was a seething mass of humanity, with what seemed like hundreds of people waiting. When I realised that my train was the next one due in and this entire bustling crowd were planning on getting on, I worked my way right down the platform but it was jam-packed. I did not know if this was a holiday, or a market day, or if the last few trains had not run. The cross-section of life was rich and varied. There were families desperately trying to stick together in the melee, children crying as their parents clutched onto them. A few red-turbaned porters scurried about with massive loads on their heads, the owners doing their best to stick with them in the crowd. Occasionally I would spy a railway employee trying to establish some kind of control. There were people with goats on leads, cages full of chickens and trolleys laden with sacks. All destined for the train slowly pulling into the platform. And it was already full!

As the doors opened a few got out but some who wanted to stay in were forced out by the pressure from inside. Those inside defended what little space they had, until someone managed to get in, and they then became part of the 'team' to prevent anyone else from boarding. People were shoving and shouting, children were crying, dogs barking. I had never experienced anything so chaotic.

'Sahib, Sahib, give me your pack.'

I saw an arm from inside reaching out, and I trusted my instincts, passed over my rucksack and managed to follow it on. People were now climbing through the windows, some had crossed to the other side of the train and were gaining entry from track side. Others were climbing onto the roof. It was the survival of the fittest, although once one member of a family was inside, somehow space was made for the rest. Even goats and baskets of chickens made it on board, but as whistles blew and the train started slowly moving forward there were still some clinging onto the outside.

This was a long train and the scene in the compartment I was in was repeated in all the others. As we moved out, the tension eased. I was squashed tight against someone who was desperate to practise his English. I tried to engage in his attempts at conversation but preferred to concentrate on breathing. Then suddenly the sack one man in the centre of the compartment was carrying on his head burst, and everyone was covered head to toe in white flour. It was thus, looking like a ghost, that I fulfilled my dream of reaching India.

CHAPTER NINE

Sikh and Ye Shall Find

My first day in India was one of the most extraordinary of the whole trip. Only a few miles from the border is Amritsar, the Sikh capital and home to their most famous and important shrine, the Golden Temple, which is built on a lake. The top two floors are covered with gold. Illuminated at night, its ethereal reflection glows on the water. It is one of the most popular tourist destinations in India, attracting more visitors in a year than the Taj Mahal. Even in late November there were still substantial numbers of people around. I checked in with the administrative offices and was allocated my space in the vast dormitory. The Sikh religion demands that all visitors, irrespective of caste, religion, ethnic origin, or social status are offered hospitality in the form of a free meal every day and a bed to sleep on.

Outside the temple complex, there was not a lot to see. I explored the markets, bought some strange-looking fruit which turned out to be delicious, and tried to get used to dealing with a new currency. It was my first experience of the Indian deep-rooted curiosity about a stranger 'Where are you from? – What is your good name? – What does your father do? – How old are you?' were questions constantly asked. In the centre of town I came across the site of the infamous Amritsar Massacre, one of the very low points in British military history when in 1919 a senior officer ordered his troops to fire upon a large group of unarmed Sikh demonstrators he had trapped in a square. With all exits blocked, hundreds were killed.

Back in the temple I joined the line of people in the vast dining room where long rows of men and women were sitting cross-legged on the floor. As one person left, another took their place. This process had been going on most of the day, feeding thousands of people.

Sikh volunteers ran this food machine, patrolling the room, placing a large banana leaf in front of a new arrival, with another following behind carrying a pot of a basic vegetable curry. A third came by with some chapattis, a fourth with rice, another with water. There was no cutlery. You ate using the chapatti to scoop up the food, being careful to only use your right hand. When you had had your fill, you upped and left, dumping your leaf in a bin and your spot was immediately filled. All this was done in remarkable silence given the numbers involved.

The Sikh faith was founded by Guru Nanak in the fifteenth century. He started writing devotional hymns and this was continued by his successors until the Sikh Holy Scripture called the Guru Granth Sahib was finalised and declared the ultimate wisdom, the embodiment of their faith. This most precious document in the Sikh religion is kept in the Golden Temple and every day the most senior of Sikh clerics take it in turns to read from it. At night, however, this holiest of artefacts is taken from the Temple and moved with great ceremony and ritual to a secure location. I was keen to see this and positioned myself in the crowd waiting for the procession to pass. I could hear the group getting closer long before I saw it. Drums were beating, and Indian trumpet-like instruments blaring. A sweeper appeared, clearing the path of any debris. Then five attendants dressed in formal Sikh attire walking ahead of the procession, one waving a sword, others carrying banners. Behind them, the

Guru Granth Sahib, the Holy Book, sat on a golden pillow on a heavily garlanded litter, like a stretcher with two long poles, carried by four large, turbaned Sikhs. Another followed behind, waving a fly-whisk over the Holy Book. It was a colourful, noisy, spectacle, but nothing had prepared me for what was about to happen.

There were a couple of people in front of me, but as he passed, one of the four Sikhs carrying the litter leant out with his free arm and grabbed my shoulder. Without saying a word he pulled me out of the crowd and gently pushed me in front of him, putting the weight of the front right corner of the litter over my left shoulder, then disappeared off into the crowd.

Hey, wait a minute! I thought. What's going on?

The other three bearers of the Holy Book had not reacted. I had no choice but to continue walking, carrying my share of the weight, moving slowly through the crowds parting in front of us, drums beating, banners waving.

I did not know whether to feel shocked or honoured. I was only concentrating on not dropping the thing. It felt like an eternity, but it was only about ten minutes later when the man reappeared and with a nod, resumed his place carrying the litter. I have asked many Sikhs who have witnessed this daily event and none have heard of anything similar. The only explanation I have is that the poor bearer was caught short and, desperately needing to visit a toilet, grabbed the first person he saw whose height nearly matched his own.

All that on my first day in the country. It made me wonder what was in store.

Delhi I found a little disappointing. It was noisy, polluted and overcrowded, and apart from the Red Fort there was not much I wanted to see or do. I was beginning to get annoyed at myself at how I was reacting to being in India. I was on the verge of shouting 'Mind your own business!' to my relentless interrogators. I was finding the country hugely materialistic, far removed from the spiritual, enlightened place I had pictured when I had set out. Also, it was tiring being constantly on guard about being ripped off. If I was honest with myself, I realised that I was not particularly enjoying the experience. Unless I could adjust my standards of personal space and privacy, things were not going to improve. What was needed was a change of attitude and this needed a change of environment. It was time to stop moving about so much and get to somewhere where I'd feel comfortable. After four days in Delhi I packed my bag and headed for Nepal.

Although Kathmandu is further south than Delhi, its proximity to the mountains, and higher altitude make it a much cooler place to be. It was now December and evenings demanded coats and scarves, and at night a good sleeping bag or duvet on the bed. Travelling there had been an adventure in itself, with armed guards protecting train carriages reserved for Westerners heading to Nepal, such had been the incidence of robberies over the last few years. Kathmandu was magical. The old wooden buildings had beautifully intricate carvings; temples seemed to dominate every street; the atmosphere was relaxed; it was easy to get about by foot or hired bicycle. Best of all were the Nepalese people. Despite having little in the way of personal possessions and living in one of the poorest countries on earth, they radiated humour and happiness.

I felt safe here. I found myself a room in a boarding house in Freak Street, home to many young travellers over the last decade. Some graffiti scribbled on the inside of the toilet door read: 'I left London because the bottom had dropped out of my world. I sit here in Kathmandu and the world is dropping out of my bottom.'

I hoped I would not share that experience.

Those were magical times. The Kathmandu dairy was just

around the corner from where I stayed and my day would start with a visit to collect an earthenware pot of fresh yoghurt which I would have for breakfast, not only because it was delicious, but also in the possibly erroneous belief that the good bugs in the yoghurt would eat any bad bugs in my stomach. Then I would explore. There was so much to see and it was ever-changing. I would spend an age on the steps of a temple at the edge of Durbar Square just watching the world go by. Sadhus, holy men with long matted hair and bright-red or white stripes across their forehead, wearing a loin cloth and carrying a staff would gather together, and I longed to know what they chatted about. I would like to think they discussed their meditation experiences or some obscure aspect of Vedic philosophy, but I suspect it was more likely to be about the tourists who stopped to take their photos, or that universal topic, the weather. Local traders carrying impossible loads would pass by, shouting out their wares. Monks, refugees from Tibet, in deep-purple robes would scuttle past immersed in conversation with each other. There was a musician selling flutes who occupied the part of the square where the acoustics were at their best, and he played the most haunting music which few stopped to appreciate. The hustle and bustle was constant. There were no vehicles in this part of the city, bicycles being the preferred form of transport. It was a daily occurrence to see a brightly decorated elephant or two being led across town by its mahout. There were a few tourists taking photos and soaking up the atmosphere, always unmolested. I never saw one being approached by anyone trying to sell them something. Of course, if they passed an open shop the owner would call out and invite them inside, but never aggressively.

Sometimes I would cycle to Pathan, the ancient capital of Nepal before Kathmandu was given that status. It was even older, the wooden-carved architecture of the main square being quite remarkable in its delicacy and beauty. Next to it was the potters' area, where thousands of small, round clay pots were drying in the sun. These were the ubiquitous throwaway teacups made from clay pulled out of the earth, fired by the sun and thrown after a single use back onto the ground, where they would soon break down into their original clay. Other times I would go and climb the steps up to the monkey temple and hang about there for a while. Or I'd wave to the Kumari, the living goddess who lives in a palace in the centre of the city. The Nepalis believe that the power of the Kumari is so strong that even a glimpse of her is believed to bring good fortune. I think she was as curious to see a Westerner as I was to see a living goddess, as she was often peeking out of her third-floor window.

There were plenty of other travellers to pass the time with and make plans. The evenings would be spent in local cafés, drinking copious quantities of tea, and, for some, smoking dope, which seemed to be condoned by the authorities. Before heading back each evening, I would always go by Durbar Square and listen to the group of musicians gathered there playing a little portable harmonium and singing devotional hymns. Not for money, not for entertainment, just for the pleasure of singing to God.

But once again I was being drawn towards the mountains. You could see them in the far distance; high, snow-clad peaks that I wanted to get in amongst. The long routes round the back of some of the main trekking areas were inaccessible for the winter, but I obtained the necessary permits to head off towards Annapurna with the intention of getting into its famous sanctuary. I took a bus to Pokhara, a journey which took all day, and deciding to enjoy the town on my way back, carried straight on to Tibetan Village, a settlement a few miles away. It was a damp, cloudy day and I had seen little, so was delighted to wake the next morning to a cloudless sunrise and a magnificent view of the snow-covered southern face of Machapuchare, the peak which looks like a fish-tail, glistening in the distance. There followed four days of ascent and descent, crossing and recrossing the raging Modi Khola River, down one side of the ever-narrowing valley then up the other. The track passed through rhododendron and higher up, bamboo forests, where I disturbed a red panda, much to the surprise of us both. I reached the last village where food and accommodation was available. It was a full day from there to the sanctuary itself, a high altitude plateau surrounded by a ring of seven thousand metre peaks, dominated by the south face of Annapurna. The weather was cloudless, the lower oxygen content of the air darkening the sky to a deep blue. I was surprised to find a tent with a young Canadian couple inside. They had come up the previous day but were off the next morning, leaving me with the place to myself.

I had hired a tent and down trousers in Kathmandu and with my duvet, jacket and four season sleeping bag I had no intention on being cold. But I was. As soon as the sun disappeared behind a mountain, the temperature dropped rapidly. I was not prepared for sleeping on top of hard-packed snow. Despite the down clothing, down sleeping bag and mat, the cold seeped through the bottom of the tent and I had a sleepless night, turning over every few minutes trying to warm up. I thawed out with the sunrise and walked higher into the sanctuary, past the lonely grave of Ian Clough, a climber killed during an expedition – the first successful ascent of the ten thousand foot south face – with Chris Bonington and Don Whillans. But when the sun started dropping I could not face another night like the last and headed down as far as the Hinko cave, where it was not the cold that bothered me, but the mice. Don Whillans claimed he saw a yeti from this cave, but if there was one around that night I was too tired to notice or to care.

Christmas was approaching, and I had arranged to meet Tony and Ursula in Kathmandu a few days before the event. I was looking forward to seeing them and to hearing their stories. I was sitting outside a café in Pokhara chatting to a couple of girls from Leeds, telling them that my parents were also coming overland and I was hoping to meet up soon. One of them, looking over my shoulder and pointing said, 'That's not your mum and dad over there is it?'

I turned to look and was amazed and delighted to see that it was. They had not noticed me, so I crept up behind them as they walked along the street.

'Change money! Change money!' I called to them as I pulled at my mother's jacket. This was a demand they must have heard a thousand times by now and rightfully ignored it. I tried another tack.

'You want some good hashish? Best quality, very cheap.' My poor attempt at a local accent seemed to work and they continued to ignore me.

Staying behind them I continued on the same tack, but moved over to my father's side.

'You want a nice young girl tonight, Sahib?'

I was pleased to see that they had learned the best tactic to deal with street hustlers and they continued to ignore me. But I was not going to give up.

'You want a young boy then?'

This was too much for my father who turned around with an angry 'Go away!' look in his face.

It took him a second to recognise me before he burst out laughing.

It was wonderful to see them and to swap stories. They had picked up messages I had left poste restante in Teheran and Kabul, and had had all kinds of adventures. They were staying in places beyond my budget, but we met up during the day, in Pokhara and then Kathmandu, celebrating Christmas with a dreadful attempt at a Christmas dinner in a local restaurant.

We booked into another guest house a few hours' bus drive east of Kathmandu and spent New Year in a small mountain village from which you could see, in the very far distance, the distinctive triangle summit of Mount Everest.

They were keen to see more of India and there was something I wanted to do in Nepal. We agreed to meet up again in Delhi in a few weeks' time before they picked up a flight home.

~

I had heard stories about a Tibetan Buddhist monastery in the Kathmandu valley. People had told me you could visit it and possibly stay there. I was curious to learn more, and having time on my hands, it seemed like an opportunity not to be missed. I packed my bags, bought a white silk scarf, which I knew was the expected gift to a Tibetan Lama, and caught a bus out of town. The monastery was not hard to find, being a large, pink building perched on top of a hill.

Kopan Monastery had been established for seven years, and was home to about forty Tibetan monks and a group of Tibetan boys who were monks in training. Some of those boys followed me up the hill, disappearing inside when I arrived at the main door. I hoped they had gone to find someone I could talk to. Sure enough, after a couple of minutes a monk appeared. We greeted each other with a 'namaste' the traditional Sanskrit greeting used throughout India and Nepal, meaning 'I bow to the God within you'.

It turned out that this monk was, with the exception of the head Lama, the only person in the place who spoke a little English.

'Is it possible to stay here?' I asked. 'I do not want to become a monk, but I would love to learn more about Tibetan Buddhism, and join in the life of the monastery for a week or two.'

The monk led me through the building, along corridors and up a flight of stairs to a door which he knocked on and went inside, indicating to me to wait there. Returning after a few minutes he said, 'The head Lama will see you now.'

The room was lit only by a number of butter-filled lamps around the walls. As my eyes adjusted to the gloom I made out a man sitting cross-legged on a raised dais, dressed in a deep-red robe over a bright yellow top. He was smiling and beckoning me forward. I greeted him in the traditional way and with outstretched arms gave him the white silk scarf I had bought for this moment. He took it and gave me one of his own from a pile by his side. Formalities over, he pointed to a cushion on the floor. I sat down, careful to avoid my feet pointing at him, which would have been a major insult.

I explained that I was interested in learning about Tibetan Buddhism, and wondered if it might be possible to spend a couple of weeks in the monastery. I wanted to get a taste of what life was like for the monks and to partake as fully as possible in the life of the monastery. The Lama understood English better than he spoke it, and after a short discussion with the monk who had met me at the door whose name was Samdup, he said I was welcome and that Samdup was happy to act as my interpreter and mentor during my stay.

We exchanged bows before I left. Although I would see him every day, I would not have an audience again with him until I was leaving in a fortnight's time.

Samdup showed me where I could leave my bag and where I would be sleeping. My bed consisted of a straw mat on the floor, one of a long line of mats in the monks' dormitory. Then I followed him to a dining room where other monks were preparing food. I was introduced to so many of his colleagues, their names and faces rapidly became a blur, but I felt welcome and reassured that I was not perceived as an intrusion. It turned out that many of them were accustomed to having Westerners around. Samdup explained that when Lama Yeshe and Lama Zopa Rinpoche, who I had just met, became refugees from Tibet in 1969, they came to the Kathmandu valley and recognised that this spot would be an excellent place to establish a base. Monks, mainly Tibetan refugees and young Nepalis, came to hear the dharma from these enlightened masters.

The first Westerners were allowed in the early seventies and now two-month retreats were held every year specifically for them. Lama Yeshe had left to teach in America and was not expected back for several months. There was not another course for foreigners for another three months, but it would be expected of me to join in with the residents in their daily activity.

Samdup's own story was fascinating and tragic. He and his brother were young novice monks in Eastern Tibet when the Chinese invaded in 1950. His parents disappeared, probably dying with tens of thousands of their fellow countryman in forced labour camps. Soon after the Dalai Lama escaped into Nepal, at a time when the Chinese were killing monks and destroying monasteries as fast as they could, the head Lama in charge of the monastery in which Samdup was living gathered together the fitter, younger monks and they set off across the Himalayas to seek safety in Nepal. It was a nightmare of a journey. They were ill-fed, ill-equipped and forced to travel mostly by night to avoid Chinese patrols across the highest, most inhospitable mountain range in the world. Frostbite and malnutrition took a dreadful toll. Twenty monks left the monastery, four made it to Nepal. The dead included the head Lama and Samdup's brother, whose bodies they had to leave where they lay on the snow.

My days at Kopan quickly fell into a pattern. It was still dark when I would rise with the monks. They would gather in the main meditation hall for the first of the day's long pujas, which I would observe. Lama Zopa, seated higher than everyone else and facing his audience, would lead the procedure, chanting ancient Tibetan texts in a deeply resonating voice which would reverberate around the room. The monks would read the texts from handwritten parchments about a foot long and three inches wide, frequently turning the leaves and occasionally joining in with the chanting. Lama Zopa directed the proceedings from his elevated seat, ringing bells or small cymbals, as well as performing intricate movements with his hands as he held various small brass objects. These sessions varied in length. The longer ones were paused for the Tibetan equivalent of a tea break. Made from tea leaves, yak butter, water, and salt, the monks loved it, but for me it was an acquired taste. My problem was that as soon as I took a sip, the little drinking bowl was again filled up to the brim. I did not realise that it was their custom to never allow a bowl to empty, and once you had had enough you simply left a full bowl beside you.

After about an hour, sometimes two, the puja would peak to a crescendo of sound before stopping abruptly, and everyone would file out in silence to the dining room for breakfast.

The first meal of the day consisted of a staple in the diet of the Tibetan people. Tsampa is made from roasted barley and mixed with a variety of other products, most commonly butter tea, to form a kind of porridge. This was consumed with much enthusiasm, noise, and mess, especially by the youngsters, who appeared ravenous. Meal over, everyone trooped out to whatever the day's duties were.

The youngsters were taken to an outside classroom where long benches were arranged in two rows. The pupils, all in their maroon monk's robes, sat facing another pupil less than a metre away from them. The teacher, an older monk, would talk to them for a short while, pacing up and down between the rows. Then, on his command, the young novices would start talking directly to the monk opposite them, one row of about twenty kids simultaneously speaking to the person opposite. This would carry on uninterrupted for about ten minutes, when, with a shout from the teacher, one row would stop talking and the other start. Another ten minutes, another word from the teacher, and then what seemed like verbal chaos would break out with every child engaging in fierce debate with the person in front of them.

Samdup explained what was happening.

'Tibetan children learn by discussion,' he said with a smile, as though recalling his own childhood. The master will give them a topic of Buddhist theory, and tell one side to defend the ideas, the other to attack them. Then they swap roles. The result is that the children grow up with the ability to debate, to see both sides of an argument, to defend their ideas, and this gives them a deep understanding of Buddhism. It's been done like this for centuries and it works.'

Some of the kids there seemed no older than ten and all were enjoying themselves. Their laughter and radiant smiles were infectious.

The rest of the day was taken up with a variety of tasks; helping in the kitchen, carting food up the hill, working in the vegetable garden, and attending classes. Many of the monks were interested in learning English. Some spoke a few phrases, but Samdup was the only one whose spoken English was good. Every day I would take an informal English class, my first and only attempt to teach English as a foreign language. Time was also put aside for studying Buddhism. Kopan had a library with some books in English, and a few hours were spent each day learning the fundamentals of the religion with Samdup always on hand to explain anything I did not understand.

It was winter but there was no obvious source of heating in the building and it was cold, especially before sunrise when we rose for the morning puja. The monks would wrap their robes tight about their bodies and hunch up against the chill. Once the sun's rays hit the building, its occupants soon warmed up. I grew accustomed to the butter tea and appreciated its warming effect in the cold, dark mornings. Halfway through the second week another couple of Westerners arrived. Showing them around, I was amazed to realise how much I had picked up in the short time I had been there.

My final duty on taking my leave of Kopan was a parting audience with Lama Zopa. Once more I was ushered into his presence and we ritually exchanged white scarves.

'What have you learned from your time here, David?' he asked.

I started talking about the Four Noble Truths and the Eightfold Path, the basic precepts of Buddha's teachings.

Lama Zopa held his hand up to stop me.

'That's all well and good,' he said, and went on to quote Buddha:

'Do not believe in anything simply because you have heard it. Do not believe in traditions because they have been handed down for many generations. Do not believe anything because it is spoken and rumoured by many. Do not believe in anything because it is written in your religious books. Do not believe in anything merely on the authority of your teachers and elders. But after observation and analysis, when you find that anything agrees with reason and is conducive to the good and the benefit of one and all, then accept it and live up to it.

'There is one lesson I would like you to take away from here,' he continued. 'One concept, which if you can live your life by it, it will transform everything you say and do.'

I was listening intently. I had come a long way to hear these words of wisdom from a Tibetan Lama.

'Imagine there is a bird that sits on your shoulder, watching, listening to all your words and actions. This bird represents your personal death. If everything you say and do is done with the awareness of your death on your shoulder, your life will be a good one. Go in peace, my friend.'

Back in Delhi a few days later I met up again with my parents. They were fit and well, having done some trekking in Nepal and spent time in Agra and Rajasthan. We had a few days together in the capital before they headed out late one evening to the airport to catch a homebound flight. It was with mixed feelings that I saw them off. I had enjoyed spending time with them in what was such a fundamentally different environment, but I was looking forward to exploring the subcontinent on my own with no schedules, timetables or deadlines to restrict my wanderlust.

CHAPTER TEN

Strange Encounters

Once again I headed north, this time to the Kumaon Himalayas, north and west of Nepal, stopping to explore places with names which resonated with tales of the Raj – Nainital, Dehradun, Mussoorie – from where in the distance the elegant peak of Nanda Devi, India's highest mountain, glowed red in the light of the setting sun. I toyed with the idea of heading off to explore the Nanda Devi Sanctuary, but a little research convinced me that this was well beyond my ability, and anyway, much of that area was out of bounds to foreigners.

Instead I went to Rishikesh where I found a room on the quieter side of the Ganges, amongst the many ashrams. I spent days walking in the surrounding hills or sitting in one of the many chai houses. Sadhus covered in ash would wander in from their hilltop caves to replenish supplies. There were few tourists. The Ganges seemed unpolluted in comparison to how it had appeared when I had crossed it further south. The air was fresh and clear. Being a holy city, it was meat and alcohol free. There was a suspension footbridge over the river, with its approaches lined by beggars, each occupying the same spot every day. I would prefer to give a few rupees to one of the ferrymen who would carry you across the river in his little boat. Some afternoons I would make my way to the ashram of my own teacher, Maharishi. Although he was seldom there, the ashram was occupied by young Indians learning to become Transcendental Meditation teachers. I would see them pacing up and down the banks of the river learning what they needed to learn, and would occasionally recognise and chat with some of the staff I had come across on the courses I had taken part in myself with Maharishi in Spain and Austria. Maharishi had created several beehive-shaped meditation cells and it was outside one of these that John Lennon had passed notes under the door to Prudence Farrow, urging her to stop meditating and come out to play.

Rishikesh felt like a spiritual home. I was meditating regularly, enjoying long, deep sessions within a few hundred yards of Maharishi's Indian base. His own teacher had been, by all accounts, a remarkable man, Brahmananda Saraswati, Shankaracharya of North India, better known within the TM organisation as Guru Dev. Maharishi had been his principle student and apprentice. There was nothing new about the practise itself. On the contrary, it came from a very ancient Vedic tradition going back many centuries to the original Shankara. Guru Dev had based himself in Jyotir Math, a small mountain village high in the Himalayan foothills, where the first Shankara and founder of this tradition had lived as a recluse in a cave. That was where I wanted to go next.

The idea of getting there was a lot easier than the reality. Bus was the only transport option, and progress up into the hills was slow and noisy. The journey took days, and in the evenings when I looked on the map I would be horrified to see how little progress had been made. The roads were tortuous, climbing ever higher, bends becoming sharper to the extent that a longer vehicle like a bus or lorry had to go forwards and backwards several times to negotiate them. Graffiti in huge letters on the road surface or cliff face extolled the virtues of careful driving, as if the huge drops over the unfenced roadside was not enough to ensure caution. But eventually, tired, hungry and travel sick, I arrived in Jyotir Math in the darkness and the rain and found a room in a hostel which I shared with a group of itinerant Tibetan traders. The next day was a public holiday and everything was closed. The following day, however, the sun was shining and my spirits rose. Guru Dev's house, the seat of the Shankaracharya for the north of India, was easy to find and his picture adorned the walls. And a few hundred yards further up the valley were the caves where the original Shankara had lived and taught in the sixth century. They were empty, and I found a spot at the back looking up towards a valley where the Ganges had its source. The snow level had descended to a few hundred feet above the town, and it would not be long before it would be blocked off for the winter. Feeling chilly, I closed my eyes to meditate at this auspicious spot.

It was not the most comfortable of places and after twenty minutes or so, I opened my eyes and stretched my legs. As I did so a group of about twelve German tourists appeared. I am not sure who was more surprised. This had been a hard place to get to and the town was distinctly lacking in any tourism provision. With them, however, was an Indian guide who explained that he was taking these people on a tour of some of the holy sites in India, especially those off the beaten track from the mainstream tourist routes. They asked me what I was doing there, and I found myself in the surreal situation, of me, a Westerner, talking to another group of Westerners about a meditation technique which was a part of the ancient Vedic tradition and which had effectively emanated from this cave.

After chatting for some time, I headed back down to the one-street town. I stopped at a chai stall and ordered up a cup of tea. As the stall holder handed it to me, the heavens opened. The man felt sorry for me standing outside in the pouring rain and, opening a flap at the side of the stall, he ushered me inside. There was nowhere to sit, just a heap of books piled up at the back.

'Sit on those,' he said, 'they are old and of no value.'

I duly obeyed. As the stall owner turned to serve another customer at his counter, I picked up one of the books I was leaning on, and flipped it open. It was a small paperback, worn at the edges and written entirely in Sanskrit. It meant nothing to me. As I dropped it back onto the pile, the front page opened to reveal a photograph of the book's author. His face I recognised immediately. It was Guru Dev.

Very little is known about this extraordinary man. Although he had been a great spiritual leader in his country, nothing of his had survived in print. But maybe this was a book about him. In itself that would be a jewel! I asked the stall-holder.

He gave the book a cursory glance, and said, 'Didn't know I had that. It was produced locally years ago; it's a book of aphorisms of Guru Dev. A local devotee wrote down the sayings and added his own commentary. You are welcome to keep it, my friend.'

Guru Dev had lived the life of a recluse before being persuaded to accept the position of Shankaracharya. The position had been unfilled for a generation as no-one had been found who was worthy enough to occupy it. He was one of the greatest spiritual leaders of the subcontinent and it was with his blessing that Maharishi came to the West with the TM meditation technique 'to spiritually regenerate the whole world'. Over the following sixty years, hundreds of thousands of people had been drawn to this, yet little was known about the man who had inspired Maharishi on to his life's mission. There were a few old photos and a short piece of black and white film. And now I held in my hand a book of all his sayings. It felt like some kind of reward for all the years of time and energy I had put into teaching TM, which had culminated outside a cave in Jyotir Math, high in the

Himalayan foothills, where the whole thing had started.

I had a basic translation made when I returned and the book is still is my possession today.

Talking to those tourists outside that cave was a turning point in my connection with the TM organisation. The technique I valued and I had enormous respect for Maharishi. I had benefited in many diverse ways from my involvement with both. But I was struggling with the direction the movement was taking. Maharishi was committed to the technique being taught in the west in pseudo-scientific terms with dubious research to justify the benefits. Then, to garner political respectability, he encouraged teachers to stand for Parliament, to seek some kind of political influence to facilitate the use of the teaching in schools, prisons, and any other government-based establishments. The 'Natural Law Party' was created, and every constituency in the UK fielded a candidate. They all lost their deposits, and I lost my faith in the organisation.

The next few months were spent criss-crossing India. I did some of the popular tourist things: Agra for the Taj Mahal at sunrise; a week in the ancient city of Benares, since renamed Varanasi; sat under the Bodhi tree at Bodh Gaya, where Buddha was enlightened; then on to the sculptures in the forest of Khajuraho, a UNESCO World Heritage site where twenty Hindu and Jain temples are covered with the most intricate and delicate carvings – the greatest artistic celebration of sexuality on earth.

I preferred to travel alone, but rarely felt lonely. When I was on the move with others it was coincidental and temporary. It was not that I did not enjoy company, more that the experience of being a stranger in a strange land was enhanced by being alone. No need to seek permission from anyone. Closer and deeper absorption into local people and places. No-one to act as a buffer between me and my surroundings. And although there was no-one to share the highs and lows with, they were, as a consequence, more intense.

Strangers are much more likely to approach a solo traveller than someone travelling as one of a pair or in a group. This created its own issues for me, specifically relating to trust. Although natural inquisitiveness is at first tiresome and intrusive, you get used to it and learn to deal with it. The offers were as constant as they were varied. Some offers were well-meant, emanating from a generous soul with a genuine desire to help – you were invited back to their homes; they would offer to accompany you to wherever you might be walking; you could bypass a queue at a railway station because their uncle worked there and would get your ticket for you; they could act as a guide, or else they would tell you that they knew much better accommodation than where you were currently staying. I had learned, however, not to trust these offers, no doubt missing out on the occasional well-meant gesture. When I went along with most of these people it was not long before I was on the receiving end of a sales pitch, which, when ignored or refused, the person would have a change of mood and get angry that I had wasted their time. But as I ventured deeper into the subcontinent I realised that there was a difference between city and country in this respect, and would be more relaxed about accepting invitations in rural areas.

Heading south, I travelled occasionally by bus but mostly by rail. 'Ticketless travel is a social evil' read the signs around the stations, and I always ensured I had a ticket but never once was asked to show it. Learning how the complex Indian Railway system worked became a necessity. The express trains which connected the cities were supposed to be the fastest, but it was not wise to use them at night. Not if you were in a hurry. These trains covered vast distances and were only supposed to stop at major cities. On one such journey it was late evening and dark outside. I was sharing a compartment with five other Indians, and wondering why the train was making sudden and frequent juddering halts, seemingly in the middle of nowhere. Each time there was banging of doors, shouting and lights disappearing across the fields into the night. I had no idea what was going on until one of the passengers in my compartment, after much peering into the darkness and frequent glances at his watch, jumped up and pulled the emergency stop cord, As the train once again ground to a sudden halt, he grabbed his bags, opened the door jumped out onto the track. The others saw the look of curiosity on my face.

'People get home quicker this way,' they explained. 'They take the faster train and use the emergency stop when they are close to their village.'

After a couple of minutes we were on our way again continuing on our stop/start progress towards the next city.

Thanks to the efforts of Indira Gandhi, Indian trains, on the whole ran quite punctually. However, one afternoon I was waiting in Puri for a train to Bhubaneshwar and it was overdue. Eventually it pulled into the station and I started to look for my name on the seat reservation list on the outside of the carriages. The stationmaster came out to help and looked at my ticket.

'I am so sorry, Sahib,' he said with a crestfallen look. 'This is yesterday's train. Today's train is running late, but it will be here soon!'

I was on a long train journey one afternoon, sharing a compartment with three other Westerners. We pulled into what was clearly a major station and I decided to stretch my legs with a walk along the platform. I asked the others to look after my rucksack and checked with a guard that the train would be in the station for at least half an hour. He gave that wiggle of the head that Indians have mastered so well to indicate yes and I stepped out into the heat and chaos of a busy Indian railway station. They are like a city in miniature. People are born, spend their lives and die in them. They support shops, traders, beggars, hustlers, thieves, an army of staff, red-turbaned porters, railway police, temples and travellers. This vast array of humanity seems to thrive in the hustle and bustle of large stations such as this. I had a couple of rupees in my pocket and I stopped at a stall to buy some fruit when, out of the corner of my eye I saw my train starting to move. To this day I have never felt such panic. I was wearing a t-shirt and shorts, flip-flops on my feet. I had given my only money to the fruit seller and the train carrying everything I needed to survive was leaving the station. My passport, all my money in traveller's cheques to see me over the next twelve months, all my clothes other than what I was wearing, disappearing away from me at increasing speed. I started to run. Indian railway stations at their quietest are busy places. This was around midday and the platform was crowded. I did my best to avoid obstacles, and felt guilty about the people I collided with, and the stalls I knocked over. I flew down the platform, oblivious to the chaos I was leaving behind. Reaching the end, I leapt onto the track where the lack of obstacles in my path allowed me to sprint as hard as I could. The train did not seem to be getting away from me, nor I any nearer. I could see the person in my compartment shouting what I thought was encouragement. I hoped they would have the sense to throw out my rucksack if I did not make it. I was aware I was running out of steam and beginning to slow down. Perhaps it was wishful thinking, but the train seemed to be slowing with me. I got close enough to grab a ring and pulled myself onto the end bumper. I was not going to be parted from my possessions.

What happened next was one of the most embarrassing moments of my life. The train was indeed slowing, and after about a hundred yards it stopped. Points clicked and clacked on the rails below and slowly we started to inch forward, returning to the station. Sitting on the buffer at the front of the train gave me an excellent vantage of the chaos I had created in my sprint along the platform. Thankfully no-one had been hurt and the overturned stalls were upright and trading again. The train had simply been changing platforms.

India seemed so vast, not like one country at all, more like dozens of interconnected states with different languages, histories, food, religions and culture, all sharing a common currency and constitution. Standing at the extreme southern tip of the subcontinent at Cape Comorin, it felt fundamentally different from the deserts of Rajasthan or the lakes of Kashmir. How the democratic process has survived in this vast country with such diverse cultures is something of a miracle.

Throughout the trip I had stayed healthy. I was vegetarian and had from the start avoided Western-style eateries, choosing local cafés in the hope that this would allow my immune system to adjust to its environment and build up resistance to whatever bugs were about. However, I was on a train to Madras when I began to feel distinctly off colour. My stomach was in turmoil. I had the rare luxury of a compartment to myself, the journey was a long one, and I used the time to sleep and meditate.

When I opened my eyes, there was one other passenger in the compartment. He presented a dramatic figure. Wearing a white silk dhoti, he had a full black beard and black hair which trailed over his shoulders. He was sitting cross-legged on the seat opposite.

'You were doing Transcendental Meditation?' he asked. He had piercing brown eyes and I got the feeling they were looking straight into my soul.

'I was,' I replied. 'How could you tell?'

He smiled and introduced himself.

'My name is Pandit Ravi Shankar,' he said. 'I have just come from being with Maharishi in Switzerland. I am on my way to Madras where I have some work to do at the TM centre there.

There are some global celebrations that Maharishi wants me to coordinate.'

Pandit Ravi Shankar was Maharishi's current right-hand man. And here he was sitting opposite me in a train heading for Madras. Our animated exchange of stories of our times with Maharishi were interrupted by my frequent visits to the toilet. Ravi Shankar said I was welcome to stay at the TM centre in Madras until I was well enough to move on. What a blessing that turned out to be.

There was something about this guy which commanded authority. The crowds at Madras station seemed to part in front of him. An empty taxi, a rarity at rush hour, stopped in front of him as we descended the steps of the station to the street. The TM centre had been donated by a wealthy Indian pop singer, and was a large house in its own extensive grounds in the city suburbs. I was shown my own ground-floor room, which had the luxury of an en suite Western-style toilet. I was going to spend a lot of time in there in the next couple of weeks!

I had dysentery and needed a restful space to recuperate. I felt so weak, I could only just manage the occasional walk in the garden before I scurried back to the toilet. But gradually I could stay out longer. Ten minutes, then half an hour, and then to go an hour without a toilet dash was a breakthrough. Then a night. Food once more became something I could contemplate.

Ravi Shankar would drop by to see how I was doing. He was overseeing a 'yagya,' an Indian ceremonial which involved a number of Brahmin priests and Vedic chanting. This was going on in a hall next to my room, and as I felt better I would wander in to watch and listen.

Eventually it was time to move on. I felt so well looked-after and had been shown so much kindness it was a wrench to leave, but I exchanged addresses, said my farewells and headed south.

Pandit Sri Ravi Shankar was to become a guru in his own

right. In the early 1980s he started his own movement called 'The Art of Living' which, thirty-five years later, claims to have reached over a hundred and fifty countries and touched the lives of 370 million people.

India had one more unexpected meeting in store for me, the most extraordinary of them all.

I was staying in an ashram in Tiruvannamalai, south of Madras, in Tamil Nadu. It was where Ramana Maharshi had lived and taught, and it was built on the side of a hill called Arunachala. Ramana Maharshi, who died in 1950, was widely regarded as one of the great Indian teachers. In his lifetime he had a huge following, including the French photographer Henri Cartier-Bresson, whose original photos taken in the ashram adorned the walls.

Arunachala is a small mountain with a distinctive shape. Tradition has it that this is where Shiva, one of the most powerful of the Hindu deities, took form on earth, and hence to the Hindu this is a very holy place. In the early morning I followed the path around the base of the hill, avoiding both the heat of the day and, usually, other people. I was surprised one morning to see an Indian also walking around the hill, but in the opposite direction. Tall and clean-shaven with short hair and slightly overweight, he wore ordinary Indian-style clothing.

Being India, there was no way we were going to pass without stopping for a chat. Our conversation ran exactly like this.

'Hello' he said.

'Hello,' I replied, waiting to be grilled about my life. I was not wrong in my assumption.

'Where are you from?' he asked in perfect English.

'From Scotland,' I answered.

He was looking at me intently. What he said next floored me. 'You are David Cooper?' It was a statement as much as a question.

My first reaction was to wonder if I had encountered some kind of mind-reading fakir, a clairvoyant with extraordinary powers.

'You do not recognise me?' he asked. 'We last met a long time ago, when I had long hair and an even longer beard.'

I looked carefully but could not place him at all.

'I am Devendra,' he said finally.

I am not often lost for words, but this left me dumbstruck. We had last met almost ten years ago in Edinburgh when he had come from India as Maharishi's representative. He had been widely regarded as the man who would take over the movement after Maharishi's death. Then, suddenly, he had disappeared from sight from the TM organisation. No-one knew what had become of him, and Maharishi never spoke of him. And here he was, an ordinary-looking man on a remote mountain path in Southern India, standing in front of me with a smile on his face. Before going to India, he was the only Indian I had met. In a country with a population of over a billion, it was an extraordinary coincidence to meet up.

After leaving Maharishi, Devendra had married and moved with his wife and mother-in-law to Tiruvannamalai. I stayed with him and his family for the next week, sleeping on his flat rooftop, enjoying his hospitality, his wonderful stories and his cooking. He was a superb chef and on my last night he cooked a complicated curry and told me why he had left Maharishi. He had had stomach cancer, and Maharishi's instructions to starve himself almost to death to rid him of his disease had proved too much, although his cancer was cured. Devendra had returned to a quiet life in India.

I left the following morning and caught a train up to Madras, then a boat, the *Chidamburam*, to Penang, in Malaysia. As India disappeared from view, I wondered what adventures lay ahead in southeast Asia.

CHAPTER ELEVEN

Snakes in the Lake

Almost immediately I regretted taking the boat instead of flying. I had bought the cheapest ticket available, which gave me a two-berth cabin in the bowels of the ship, but no access to the upper decks where there was a small swimming pool. I was sharing a cabin with a German who spoke little English. The lack of air conditioning in the lower decks made the boat unbearably hot and stuffy, but it was the dining arrangements which were the most depressing. The third class passengers consisted of about twenty Westerners and several hundred Indians, and we all ate together in one vast dining room. The food was always the same, no variation or choice, irrespective of what meal it was. Curry and rice. Take it or leave it. No utensils were provided as we were expected to eat in the Indian way only using our fingers.

However, the crew felt sorry for us and we were given the option of eating Western-style food after the Indian passengers had been fed, and it was brought down to us from the kitchens which served the upper decks. They also turned a blind eye to us using the facilities of the first and second class passengers, in particular the outside pool. The crossing was not going to be that bad after all. We made one brief stopover on the remote Nicobar Islands before finally arriving at Penang, seven days and seventeen hundred nautical miles after leaving India.

Penang is an island with George Town its capital. I found it charming, with a strong colonial feel, British-influenced architecture, interesting shops and stalls where food was good, cheap and plentiful. The people were friendly and spoke English as though it was their mother tongue, albeit with an old-fashioned vocabulary. I found a place to stay on a street close to the sea called Rope Walk, and spent a week there before moving out of town to a kampung – a traditional village of houses on stilts. I found a room at 'Bob's Place', run by a Filipino who had been a POW of the Japanese. He rented out rooms to young Western travellers and provided food and entertainment in the form of stories about his long and eventful life.

Penang has an eclectic mix of religions which co-exist quite happily. The colonial period left a strong Christian community, while the rural Malay were animists who believed in the sanctity of every living thing. The huge Chinese population also believed in the presence of a strong spirit world, and had miniature houses outside their own homes where they would burn incense and leave offerings to appease ghosts. There was a smaller Muslim presence, the followers of Islam being far more dominant in the eastern half of the country, but there was also a large Hindu population. There were many temples in George Town, and the most famous, right in the middle of the island, was a sanctuary for snakes. There were hundreds of them, most extremely poisonous, all venerated by the Hindu priests and encouraged to be there. I am not fond of snakes, and they were everywhere you looked. I wondered if the strong, constant smell of incense had a soporific effect, as it was maintained that no visitor or temple priest had ever been bitten.

One afternoon the peace of the village was broken by a lot of banging of drums, blowing of small Indian trumpets and loud chanting. I wandered out to see what was happening. There were about a dozen men walking in single file, each with large steel spikes or hooks attached to their bodies. The spikes were over a metre long and had either been pushed through both cheeks, or vertically, through their tongues. Others had hooks passed through a thick fold of flesh on their backs, with the other end attached to carts which they were pulling along the ground, stretching their skin far out from their bodies. There was a crowd following this unusual procession, and the noise was tumultuous. This was apparently a Hindu celebration which involved these men performing some kind of penance. The whole operation was overseen by Hindu priests who would only proceed with piercings when they were happy that the person had entered a trance state and would feel no pain. It was a strange sight and after a couple of hours the metal work was removed with no apparent sign of any harm to the flesh.

Eventually I moved on to explore more of the country, spending a few days in Kuala Lumpur, and a few more visiting tea plantations in the Cameron Highlands, before heading back to Penang from where it was a short cheap flight to Medan in Sumatra, the largest of the Indonesian islands.

In complete contrast to Penang, Medan was the most unpleasant place I had ever been to. It was hot, a sticky, humid heat which sapped energy. Perhaps because of the open sewers, there were so many flies it was difficult to breathe without taking in a mouthful. The combination of the odour of sewage and plentiful durian fruit, which on their own smell like a busy public toilet which has not been cleaned for six months, encouraged me to head straight for the station, but there was no train to my destination until the next day, and I was forced to spend a sweaty, sleepless night in this depressing town.

For Western travellers of my age group wandering around Asia in the seventies there were certain destinations to which we were drawn, about which we were able to pick up reliable and relevant information from fellow travellers. These places tended to be isolated, surrounded by natural beauty and lacking the trappings of major tourist destinations; though off the beaten track, cheap accommodation and good food were readily available. The rule of thumb seemed to be that the more effort required getting there, the more uncomfortable the journey, the more worthwhile it was to make the effort. Samosir Island in the middle of Lake Toba in central Sumatra fitted the bill perfectly, and that was where I was heading next.

I was now using Tony Wheeler's *Asia on a Shoestring* as my travel bible and despite his warnings about bus travel in Sumatra, I was just not prepared for the reality. Indonesians are not a tall people and their buses are designed accordingly. The hard, right-angled seats would have been uncomfortable for anyone, but for my six feet frame it was nigh on impossible to fit into the available space. The only two options for me were the front seat or the seat in the middle of the back row, and if these were not available I had to lie along the floor. The buses did not seem to follow a timetable, and only departed a town when they were overflowing with people. I had no choice but to leave my rucksack on the roof, where, at the first stop I found someone rifling through to see what they could find. That was when I decided that I too would ride with the luggage on the roof, where I could at least stretch my legs.

Outside Medan the roads soon deteriorated to a single-track, rutted and potholed nightmare. Mostly we travelled at little more than a walking pace. Major breakdowns were common, and showed just how much experience, skill and ingenuity the drivers had in dealing with the mechanics of these ancient vehicles. We broke down for the fourth or fifth time, stuck in the middle of a large puddle about thirty yards long. Everybody was expected to get out and push the bus out of the water. As I was about to climb off the roof, I noticed a snake, about six feet long, slide out of the grass and into the puddle. I was the only person who had seen it. I was wearing shorts and sandals, and there was no way I was getting in to the water. I pointed and shouted, 'There's a snake! There's a snake in the water!' but no-one spoke any English. I tried in vain to indicate by sign language. So, on the roof I stayed, the only person who did not get off the bus and into the snake infested water. The only white person on board, sitting alone on the roof as the other passengers pushed and heaved the bus onto dry land.

The hundred and fifty mile journey took eighteen hours. Arriving in Prapat on the northern shore of Lake Toba it was too late to catch a ferry over to Samosir Island. I was just too tired to find somewhere to stay and slept on a bench beside which the morning ferry would arrive. It was a peaceful night, very different from a night at this spot some seventy thousand years ago which saw the biggest explosion on the planet. The Toba volcanic eruption has been described as apocalyptic, hundreds of times bigger than anything experienced in recent history. It covered South Asia in ash, created a volcanic winter, caused a drop in global temperature, and a severe reduction of the humanoid population of the world. The lake that sits in the volcanic caldera is the largest of its kind. Fortunately, it was quiet and peaceful as I crossed to Samosir Island the following morning.

The Toba Batak people are a largely Christian community who live in wooden houses with steep upturned ends on the roofs, not unlike an upturned boat. A few of these houses were available as 'losmen', cheap accommodation in a small family house which had put aside a room or two where people could stay. You got a room, bed and mosquito net, and use of a bathroom in which was usually a large, square container full of water. This was not something you would climb into, but rather extract water from with the bucket provided and throw that over you as a makeshift shower. There was no mains electricity or vehicles. The island was lush green with paddy fields, many and varied fruit trees, and an abundance of wild flowers. The surrounding scenery was beautiful, with mountains on the mainland opposite and verdant hillsides covered in dense green jungle behind. It was not surprising that these Toba Batak people were amongst the happiest folk I have ever come across. And they loved to sing. Whether it was working in the fields, out on the fishing boats, walking to the markets, or cooking in the kitchen, they sang, very melodiously. It was almost impossible, in daylight hours to be outside and not hear at least one person singing. Working, or walking in company they would sing in glorious harmonies. At church on a Sunday they could compete with a Welsh choir. This was a delightful place. The icing on the cake was the quality of the fresh food available. Vegetables from the gardens, fish from the lake, fruit from the jungle, and all costing almost nothing. They even grew their own coffee, the best I had ever tasted.

After a week in this isolated paradise I set off to walk across the island. This was going to take a couple of days and involved climbing three thousand feet to an escarpment which dominated the middle of the island, travelling across it, and down to the coast on the other side. There was a path through the jungle and a village in the middle of the plateau, where someone would find me a bed for the night. I took a large staff with me as security against any wildlife and was grateful for it when I encountered a large male boar on the path in front of me. As surprised and alarmed as I was, it hastily disappeared into the undergrowth. After a night with a family in a village in the middle of the island I carried on to the other coast and made my way back to base by boat with some local fishermen.

My Indonesian visa was only valid for a month and there were other places I wanted to go. Lake Toba is close to the equator and was the most southerly point of my journey. It was time to turn north and start heading home.

I stopped in the town of Berastagi for a few days, just long enough to climb Mount Sibayak, a seven thousand foot high volcano still regarded as active, although it had not erupted for a hundred years. You had to tread carefully to avoid the steam vents blowing off like a pressure cooker at the summit. The smell of sulphur was overwhelming, but the hot springs were good to relax in on the way down.

I was staying in a family-run guest house, where the owner, Mr Pelawi spoke English well enough to teach local children in his house in the evenings. The sounds from his class would perforate through the thin walls and on occasion he would ask me to join in and talk to his students. On my third day he took me to a local traditional wedding of the Karonese people, the largest tribal group in the area. This was a drawn-out affair involving hundreds of guests and much sitting around doing little, before vast amounts of food was consumed. It was unusual for outsiders to be asked to these occasions and I was treated as an honoured guest, to the extent that, despite my protestations, I was included in all the wedding photographs. The ancient camera clicked and whirred and somewhere on the island there will be fading wedding pictures of the happy couple with a stranger towering above them. I was told that my presence was an omen of good fortune for the couple. I hope that was right.

I asked my host more about these fascinating people. The Karonese are a clan-based society, with their own language. Nineteenth-century Dutch missionaries converted them to Christianity, but many incorporated their old animist belief in ghosts, spirits and traditional jungle medicine. My anthropology training was kicking in and I was curious to learn more. It turned out that Mr Pelawi had connections with a Karonese village where the people still lived in traditional longhouses. He gave me a letter to give to the headman of this place and detailed directions involving a bus journey and a ten-mile hike through paddy fields and grasslands.

I realised I was getting close when I first heard, then saw a number of children playing in the fields, their mothers nearby working the paddy fields, planting rice. The kids ran along beside me, leading me into a cleared area containing twenty thatched wooden buildings on stilts. The floor level was about ten feet off the ground, on top of a complex framework of uprights from tree trunks and an interlocking wood beam framework. From here the walls sloped outwards at an angle of forty-five degrees, meeting a steeply angled thatched roof which peaked at a double pointed top about fifty feet from the ground. Although described as longhouses they appeared to be shaped more like a square and each roof was topped with an impressively horned water buffalo skull, placed there to ward off evil spirits. The communal village house was even more impressive and complex, with open sides supported on each of the four sides by fifteen wooden pillars about two metres apart. The steeply sloping thatched roof, interrupted by another set of vertical wooden pillars, was covered with star-shaped apexes, and again topped with buffalo skulls.

The brother of the village chief had been summoned by the kids as he was the only person there who spoke English. He saw me gaping at these beautiful constructions.

'There is not a nail in any of them,' he proudly exclaimed. 'These houses are built and maintained by ourselves using techniques handed down by our forefathers.'

Followed by a gaggle of curious children, we walked through paddy fields, and cinnamon and maize crops as he told me more about the place and their customs.

Each longhouse housed up to eight families. There were no internal walls, but each family unit knew where their space stopped and their neighbours' started. There were small alcoves within each family space where the adults slept. Each family cooked for themselves on their own open fire. Children stayed with their family units until puberty, when they were moved to single-sex longhouses where they would live until they married. This was a patriarchal society, where the power and authority resided with the husband of the family. The village chief held a hereditary position that gave him absolute secular authority, but the man who had all the power over spiritual matters was the village shaman, in Indonesia and Malaysia known as the dukun. Dukuns had a variety of duties, primarily to do with healing. Using herbs, offerings, plants, animal sacrifice or exorcism, these men were the first port of call for anyone afflicted with an illness. Their skills extended to sorcery, the use of charms and blessings, soothsaying and dealing with the spirits of the dead. In the Karonese culture the dukun would exhume a body seven years after its death, remove the skull, enter a trancelike state and start talking with the voice of the dead person, guiding and advising what the deceased's family should be doing. Although these practices were banned by Indonesian law and run contrary to Christian and Islamic belief, they were, and apparently still are, common practice amongst rural communities.

After being shown what part of the river was the male area to wash in, I was eventually led into the main longhouse where I was going to spend the night. Space was made for my sleeping bag in the chief's family area, which had his brother and his family on one side, and the dukun and his family on the other. I counted nearly fifty people under the one roof, occupying a large open space, with eight separate meals being prepared and consumed, children being settled down to bed, dishes cleared and cleaned, and yet not only was the noise minimal, but the sense of peace palpable. With the chief's brother-in-law translating, I talked for a long time with the dukun. He was an ordinary-looking man, about ten years older than me. He had learned his skills from his predecessor and was happy to talk about what he did. He sensed my interest, and asked if I wanted to train as a dukun myself, a process that would take a couple of years and involve learning the language. This was a career path I was not planning to follow, but I thanked him, before settling down for the night.

On Lake Toba I had heard about another place deep in the Sumatran jungle where there was a sanctuary for orangutan. The nearest village to this was Bukit Lawang and this was my next stop. I arrived in the village in the late afternoon and found a losmen to stay in, before going for a swim in the river around which the village was built. This same river was to wipe out the village and kill most of its inhabitants in four years' time, when a flash flood, caused by illegal logging upstream, would create a twenty-metre high tidal wave. There were no other visitors; the nearby sanctuary was yet to become a popular tourist destination.

The man who ran the losmen in which I was staying invited me to join him and his family at a gathering in the communal village hut that evening. As we headed along the path to get there after dinner, we heard a deep-throated roar coming from deeper in the jungle.

'That was a tiger,' my host explained. 'We never see them, but we hear them at night quite often.'

Most of the village had reached the communal hut before us. It was the only building in the village which had electricity, powered by a generator humming in the background. I wondered if I had been invited to a village celebration. There were lots of children sitting on the floor below a low platform and dozens of adults packed into the rest of the thatched, open-walled shelter. The hubbub of voices dropped as a man climbed onto the makeshift stage and uncovered a television, switched it on, and for the next hour the entire population of this remote village deep in the Sumatran jungle watched the last episode of popular American soap *Dallas.*

I left the village on foot the following day and walked along a clear path through dense jungle. Rivers were crossed by means of a boat attached to a self-operated pulley system. I felt a little apprehensive as this was an alien environment. Every noise from the dense green all around gave me a fright. Then, suddenly, as I rounded a corner on the jungle track there appeared, about five yards in front of me, an orangutan.

'Stop there!' a man wielding a big stick called out as he appeared from behind the big ape. The orangutan was curious, however, and came closer to me, but the man scurried up to it and hit it hard with his stick. The beast reached for a branch and swung up into a tree.

'Welcome,' the ranger said to me. 'Come.' He led me further along the path to a clearing where there were several platforms built in the trees.

He picked up on my look of surprise at the way he had handled the orangutan.

'Tigers are their only predator and they are too heavy to climb the jungle trees,' he explained. 'The orangutans normally never touch ground, but they have lost this instinct because they have been in captivity. We have to retrain them to never go on the ground again, and when we see them on the ground we hit them as hard as we can. It's for their own safety, otherwise a tiger will get them for sure.

'All the apes here have been captured by local people when young and taken in small cages in terrible conditions. We hear about them and take them back to the jungle where we are training them to fend for themselves. These adult orangutans are still not quite capable of finding their own food, which is why we feed them twice a day. Eventually we take them by helicopter to a very remote part of the jungle and release them.

'We also have to try to re-instil their natural fear of humans, so please do not go near the animals, and if one approaches you, back off and call one of us.'

An English woman working at the centre spent some time telling me what they were doing and the plans for the place to become a major orangutan rehabilitation centre and a tourist attraction in its own right.

These apes were not restricted in their movement but chose to stay there because of the food supply. I spent a couple of hours watching a dozen fully grown orangutans playing together in the trees of the Sumatran jungle before heading back.

Returning to the Tye Ann Guest house in Penang, I bought my ticket home from a hustler called 'Fast Eddy', a black Indian man who had an office in the courtyard of the nearby New China Hotel. He was one of those dealers who could get you anything and for some reason I trusted him. I asked about him when I was back in Penang twenty years later and I was told he had become a major player in the Malay black market but had been stabbed to death in a fight protecting his territory. He had sold me a perfectly valid ticket for a flight out of Bangkok scheduled for six weeks' time. I took the train north, out of Malaysia and into Thailand.

On the travellers' grapevine, I heard about a group of islands off the east coast of Thailand which had pristine beaches and no tourists. The nearest mainland town was Surat Thani, and it was there that a small group of us got off a train and headed down towards the shoreline. It was eight p.m. and dark. We found a fisherman who, with his crew, was preparing to go out on his boat with his nets on a night's fishing trip, and persuaded him to take us to Koh Samui, the island we were aiming to get to. There was a public ferry but it was intermittent and unreliable.

We arrived in the early morning, jumped off the boat and waded ashore carrying our gear above our heads to keep it dry. We were in the main town, which was small and everyone was still asleep. Eventually the place stirred to life and we got a lift to a beach on the other side of the island, a place called Lamai. There was a communal open kitchen area and six small thatched huts on stilts at the top of the beach. I was shown to an empty one. The roof and walls were made from interwoven palm tree leaves. No furniture, but there was a bare electricity bulb attached to a wire which ran along the ceiling and a small coir mat on the floor. This was going to be home for the next three weeks and I was as happy as could be.

The beach was picture-postcard perfect. The local coconut farmer had created a small business sideline by providing food in the open kitchen area and bar he had set up on the sand. There were about a dozen people staying there and many lazy days were spent on the beach, in the water, and exploring other parts of the island. There were plenty of other identical beaches, nearly all of them deserted.

I heard a scrabbling on the floor of my hut one night, and switched on my torch to see three scorpions scurrying close to my head. I squashed them with my shoe, but spent a sleepless night watching and listening out for any more. In the sea that day a shark appeared, probably totally harmless, but big enough to give me a fright. And earlier that afternoon, resting in my hut avoiding the heat of the midday sun, I glimpsed a movement above my head in the palm fronds which formed the ceiling. There was a cobra slowly making its way in my direction. It was between me and the door, and the only sensible escape route was to crash through the end wall of the hut to land ignominiously on the beach. The coconut farmer thought this was hilarious and didn't mind that I had destroyed his hut. The snake was chased away and the hut rebuilt, but the place, with its scorpions, sharks, and snakes had begun to lose its charm and it was time to move on.

Bangkok was hot, humid, dirty, noisy, and by the standards

I was used to, expensive. I was thankful that Fast Eddy's ticket was valid and it was with a sense of relief that I boarded the Jordanian Airlines flight out of Thailand to the Middle East.

Arriving from Bangkok in Jordan's capital Amman after so many months travelling made me an obvious target, and I was taken to one side at customs and hustled into an office where a fat, plain-clothes customs official started going through my bag.

His English was not good, but he had decided that he did not like me.

After emptying my pockets he started on my rucksack, which had a pile of dirty clothes at the top. Undeterred, he continued on until he came to a washbag. Inside he found some paracetamol, clearly labelled as such.

'What's this?' he cried out in glee.

'It's in case I get a headache from talking to people like you,' I replied. I knew his English was not good enough to understand my rudeness.

'It's LDS!' he exclaimed. 'I know it is. It's LDS!'

Foolishly I said, 'Might you mean LSD?'

'Yes, yes,' he replied, quite agitated by now. 'That's it, LSD.'

Fortunately, his colleague pointed out that this was in a sealed and labelled packet just the same as would have been available on a local market. Having been detained for about an hour, I was finally allowed into the country.

I made use of an offer of accommodation in the city from an English couple I had met on the plane. They had a city centre apartment, and they helped me obtain the right paperwork to visit the Occupied Zone of the West Bank of Jordan, aka Israel, but first there was a very ancient ruined city about one hundred and fifty miles south of Amman which I was hoping to get into.

The Nabateans were an Arab people who lived in Northern Arabia and whose origins can be traced back to an age well before Christ. Their greatest legacy was to create the city of Petra in the first century BC. Although there is evidence of occupation of the area going back to prehistoric times, the Nabateans built, or half built, half carved, this city out of solid rock. Described as one of the greatest, largest and most important archaeological sites in the world, the site remained unknown to the West until a European explorer stumbled across it in the early nineteenth century. Famously described by John Burgon as 'a rose-red city half as old as time', it was now on my doorstep and I was keen to visit. I found a bus which dropped me off about half a mile from the entrance.

Perhaps because of the political instability of the area, there were no tourists to be seen. I waved away an unhappy-looking Arab who was trying to sell a ride on his camel down to the entrance, and instead set off on foot along the Siq, a deep split in the rocks which, at the entrance to the city, is narrow enough to touch both walls. The kind of place a man could defend against an army. As you emerge, you get your first view of Petra's most famous ruin, 'The Treasury', a forty-metre high, columned, two-storey building, beautifully carved out of solid rock. As I walked further into the valley it became apparent that Petra covered a huge area. On both sides there were many more buildings, caves, amphitheatres, tombs, temples, and the remains of what had been an intricate water management system, all carved from the rock.

Although there were no other visitors, I did not have the place to myself. Both in and around many of the caves there appeared Bedouin families for whom this was home. One approached me and asked in broken English where I was from. We chatted as best we could for a few minutes and when I asked if I could leave my gear somewhere safe for the day, he pointed to a cave and said it would be fine there.

Unencumbered with a backpack I spent the day exploring, wishing I had bought a guidebook. I had no idea what I was looking at or whose tomb I was in, but the place had an atmosphere of ancient history about it which left me with a sense of awe.

It was late afternoon before I headed back to where I had left my pack. The man I had spoken to earlier wandered across and I asked if it might be possible to stay the night. A hot meal would be out of the question but I had enough food with me to keep me going for at least another day. As it was, I need not have worried. The Bedouin have a deep-rooted sense of hospitality to strangers, and I was shown an empty cave adjacent to one occupied by a family. It was on an easily accessed ledge about a third of the way up the cliff face. The family kindly brought me food which I ate watching the sun set, its rays making the cliffs opposite glow a beautiful red, catching the colour of the sandstone and magnifying its hue. Lights appeared in caves on either side of the divide. Clearly there was quite a large Bedouin population here, but it was only the lights that gave their presence away – the quality of silence was profound. Sitting at the entrance I tried to absorb the atmosphere, willing it deep into my being as I knew I would never experience anything quite like this again. I tried to imagine what this place had been like over the millennia it had been occupied, and the vision that the Nabatean elders had to execute such constructions from the existing cliffs. According to Arab tradition, this was where Moses struck a rock with his staff and water came forth. I wondered if he had appreciated the same view I was enjoying. Then along came the Romans and built an amphitheatre again out of solid rock, which six thousand people could occupy. And later, much later, Laurence of Arabia had stayed here, who knows, maybe in this very cave.

'Howdy mate, you all right?' A woman dressed in Bedouin clothes had entered the cave and was standing in front of me, interrupting my flow of thoughts and my view. She spoke with a broad Australian accent.

'I heard there was a Pom staying here! I thought I'd come say hi, and see if there is anything you need.'

We spoke for a while and she told me she had come travelling here a few years ago and had never left. Now married to a Bedouin man, she was happy in her life with these nomadic people.

I explored the area more the next day, before leaving in time to get to the nearest pick-up point for a bus back to Amman.

Leaving Jordan was relatively straightforward. Entering Israel on the other side of the Allenby Bridge over the River Jordan was where the fun started.

Four and a half hours later, after I had been interrogated by three different people as to why I was visiting Israel, after my passport had been checked and double-checked in different offices, after I had been photographed and fingerprinted, and after my luggage had been x-rayed, then emptied in front of me, and everything that could be opened was minutely searched, I was finally allowed into the country and put on a bus to Jerusalem. Each bus was allocated a tourism officer to answer any questions about the country. He was apologetic about the rigorous entry procedure, but it was understandable given the political atmosphere at the time. I was dropped off at the Haifa Gate, one of the entrances to the old part of the city. I found a guest house called Alice's Place, my base for the next fortnight. Plenty time to do the usual tourist things – the Wailing Wall, the Temple Mount and the narrow market streets of the historic and troubled city. Time to see a bit of the country – Bethlehem, Nazareth, Galilee. Time to swim in the Dead Sea, stay in a kibbutz called Amiad near Tiberius and watch the sunrise from the top of Masada Rock, where the Romans laid siege to a Jewish settlement for four years, where the besieged committed mass suicide when they knew they were going to be overwhelmed.

My money was now almost gone. I had enough to get back to Jordan and to get to the airport to pick up the rest of the flight home. Back in Scotland eleven months after I had left, I was completely broke. I had hoped a trip of this magnitude would quell my wanderlust, but I couldn't help planning the next one on the flight back.

CHAPTER TWELVE

You Can't Eat the Scenery

'David, wake up, wake up! There is a fantastic full moon.'

My sister Jo was calling at my bedroom door, it was just after two a.m. on a cold December morning. I was staying with her and her husband Alan in a modern bungalow overlooking the shores of Loch Garry, near Glengarry in the heart of the Scottish Highlands. This was Alan's aunt's house, and she was newly resident in a home for the elderly and unlikely to return. Alan and Jo had moved in to look after the place.

Jo appreciated my interest in photography and did not want me to miss the opportunity of a good shot.

'Thanks, Jo,' I yawned, resisting the temptation to go back to sleep. The crystal-sharp moon was full, hanging just above the top of the snow-capped mountain at the head of the loch and perfectly reflected on the still black water. The effort to get my camera gear sorted and face the cold was worthwhile. The resulting photo became a postcard and was bought by the Edinburgh Woollen Mill, who enlarged it to fill a wall in each of their nationwide chain of shops.

As I was erecting the tripod, attaching the camera and fiddling about with filters, about half a mile away on the hillside opposite, from a van parked in a lay-by, I was being observed, photographed, and my movements recorded. It would be some months before I discovered why.

Six months had passed since I returned from Asia. Finding work in Edinburgh had been easy enough. I applied for three locum social work jobs, was offered them all, and accepted one with the Leith Social Work Office where I concentrated on short-term work with offenders. I was really enjoying being there and my work colleagues were delightful. In particular was a lovely, sparkly, brown-haired, blue-eyed girl called Lin, who had a great sense of humour and an infectious laugh, with whom I started a relationship. We would often escape the city for weekends away and it was on one such weekend that we had gone to stay with my sister.

Some weeks later I was up in Loch Garry again, having accepted Jo's kind invitation to spend Christmas with them and their four daughters. It was one of those magical Christmases, dry, sunny, crisp and cold. The loch and glen glowed like a Christmas card, with ice, frost, sunshine and mountains covered in snow and ice. The girls had been given new bikes and were thrilled. We spent time outside teaching them how to ride and remained oblivious once again of the van in the lay-by on the hill opposite. But I did notice the cracks which had appeared on the ceiling of the sitting room. The loft ladder access had been padlocked, 'to stop the girls going into the attic to play,' said Alan. 'It might be dangerous up there.'

Just how dangerous was soon to become apparent.

February, a few weeks later, and it had been a busy day at work in the Leith Social Work Office. I had been the duty officer and there had been an incident involving child protection which had been difficult and emotionally draining. I was looking forward to a relaxing evening in my Buccleuch Place flat, but there was a surprise in store. Waiting for me in the flat were my sister and her four daughters.

Jo looked exhausted. She would never turn up at my door

without some pre-arrangement. Something must have happened. Together we made up beds and settled the girls. I opened a bottle of wine, and prepared some food. Over the course of the evening, my sister told me her story.

Jo and Alan had been farming on Kerrera for the past seven years. On the surface the lifestyle was idyllic: making a living from the land in a beautiful location.

'But you can't eat the scenery,' said Alan to a BBC crew making a documentary about the crisis in Scottish hill farming. Alan and Jo had been struggling to get by in what were tough circumstances. Although Alan was skilled at his work, much of the land on the farm was too steep and rocky to graze animals or grow anything. What there was he managed well, introducing the right breed of cattle to suit the harsh conditions and managing his sheep stock to ensure the best prices when it came to market day. But being island-bound, expenses and transport costs were high. Never a day off, never a holiday, just hard physical work in all weathers. Being a tenant on a small-holding, no possibility of employing any help, trying to raise four daughters, cash always tight – it was a demanding, arduous existence.

Both Jo and Alan were well suited for this life. Jo had spent much of her early childhood holidays living in basic conditions on Scottish islands. After marrying Alan she had lived and worked in remote communities in Zambia and Fiji, raising their ever-expanding family where there was no mains electricity or fresh running water. Alan Grey came from a large family with some illustrious forebears including a Prime Minister, a Foreign Secretary, assorted Earls, Ladies and Lords, and a President of the Hudson Bay Company. He was one of eight siblings, and when his father died at an early age, his mother worked as many hours and jobs as she could to have her children privately educated.

After their third daughter was born in Fiji, the couple decided that it was time to find work in the UK, and when the farm on Kerrera became available, it was the perfect opportunity for them. Jo opted for a home birth for their fourth child, another daughter, the first child born on the island for many years.

Alan is a quiet man, tall, thin, soft-spoken, bearded and bespectacled. He has an air of gentle intelligence and trustworthiness, someone with whom you could share a secret. Perhaps it was not surprising that he was approached one New Year's Eve by Stuart Prentiss, who, along with Mike Shaw, was renting a house on the remote western shore of Kerrera. They were running a yacht charter business using a forty-foot schooner, *Bagheera,* and a yacht called *Salamander.*

Seeing Alan on his own, Prentiss seized the opportunity to approach him discreetly.

'That boat we have, Alan,' he said, 'Well, what if I told you it was a front for a different type of operation? I am involved with others importing grass from Columbia, and we could use your help. We are especially interested in your aunt's house in Glengarry. It's empty and remote, ideal for our purposes.'

Alan was old enough for the swinging sixties to have passed him by, but he knew that when they were talking about grass they did not mean cattle feed. He was being asked to allow his aunt's house to be used a storeroom. Although aware of the risk, he was persuaded that this was going to be an easy, safe operation, involving large quantities of a soft drug. The reward on offer would be the answer to his precarious financial position.

'What do you want me to do?' he asked. He was in.

Over the next couple of months Alan helped with the offloading from the schooner and loading into vans, sometimes on Kerrera, where the beach at Barnambuc on the remote west coast of the island was the drug smugglers' dream location. Isolated and private, with a beach exposed to Loch Linnhe where ocean-going tugs full of grass could moor off, the bales offloaded onto large, fast, seven-metre zodiac rigid inflatables which could land on the beach. The alternative drop-off point was the lonely Conaglen, near Fort William, where an ocean-going trawler from Columbia offloaded her illegal cargo, in the form of bales, each about the same size, weight and shape as a bale of hay. Some fifteen tons of high-grade marijuana arrived like this, most of which was driven to stashes in England, but five tons were stored in the Glengarry house.

The person behind the operation was Howard Marks, a man who was to become Britain's most notorious drug importer. After his undergraduate days at Oxford, Marks met up with an Irish petty criminal called James McCann, a member of the IRA, an escapee from the infamous Crumlin Road Prison, an ex-con of Parkhurst Prison on the Isle of Wight and, at the time they met, on the run from the Irish Republic. Because of his Irish connections, McCann was of interest to MI6. They were aware that Marks was in contact with this man, and in 1972 he was recruited as a spy by Her Majesty's Government to feed back any relevant information about McCann. Marks had been working with McCann successfully importing cannabis into Ireland from Pakistan, but in 1973 he was arrested on a minor drugs charge, for possession of barely enough to make a joint. Marks jumped bail, and he and McCann disappeared off the radar for the next seven years.

The newspapers made a meal of the story, suggesting amongst other things that the pair of them had been executed by the IRA. But the reality was different. With the help of forty-three aliases, twenty-five false companies and eighty-nine separate phone lines, Marks had created an extensive international network dedicated to the illegal importation of marijuana and cannabis. He also ran a successful legitimate business, an Oxford boutique called Annabelinda, and for a time was the manager of the seventies pop star P.J. Proby. Living off his not inconsiderable wits, he continued to import soft drugs from Asia, into Ireland and on to mainland UK.

Then Marks changed his source to Columbia, and the destination to the west coast of Scotland. Kerrera was not the only operation he had going on, but it was by far the biggest. The Columbian connection was new, and Marks' suppliers, operators from a cartel on the other side of the Atlantic, grew suspicious that their goods were not meeting sales targets. One was sent over to investigate. But he was known to drug enforcement agencies, and was being followed. He was seen meeting Stuart Prentiss, who in turn was followed up to the west of Scotland, where all the people he met with were identified.

Customs and Excise officials were duly alerted to the likelihood of drugs being imported into the country in the Oban area. Details were scant, but names and places were suggested, and officers dispatched to the west coast.

Prentiss realised he was being followed, and alerted the rest of those involved that the authorities were onto them. They set about destroying what evidence they could, burning the inflatables and chucking what grass was still on Kerrera into the sea.

But the bales did not sink. They drifted with the tide until they were washed up on the east coast of Mull, at a place appropriately called Grass Point.

Recognising what the bales were, a curious beachcomber alerted the authorities. The people Alan was in touch with went to ground. He was left with three tons of grass in his attic. And he was being watched.

Shortly after, the authorities raided three houses where they suspected drugs were being stored. Two of these were in England, the third was Glengarry. A total of fifteen tons of grass had been found, to this day the largest volume of drugs found in a single operation in Europe. Alan had been arrested; Jo was not held to have had any responsibility and allowed to go on her way. She packed for herself and the girls and came down to Edinburgh.

'Where are you going to go?' she was asked by a customs official.

'To my brother David in Edinburgh,' she replied.

'Oh yes, he's the guy who wanders about outside in the middle of the night taking pictures, isn't he? We know all about him.'

I was astounded to hear Jo's story. I had had no idea what had been going on, but it did explain the strange clicking noises I heard every time I had recently used my telephone. The following morning it was headline news. A legal contact told us that Alan had been formally charged and transferred to London where he was on remand in Brixton prison.

Those were grim months for Alan. A long way from home, isolated from his friends and family, and abandoned by the people who had got him into this position. He was fully cooperative with the authorities, taking responsibility for his role in the affair, and his role as a minor bit player, a storekeeper, was accepted. Nevertheless, he would face trial with the others.

He was on remand for a year before the trial began. Held in Number One court of the Old Bailey, its daily proceedings were front page news. Alan was found guilty and duly sentenced to four years imprisonment. He spent a year in Ford Open Prison in Kent before he was released.

For Howard Marks, it was a different story. He presented himself as a dynamic, intelligent person with an anti-authoritarian streak. His defence centred on the idea that he was in the employ of the Mexican drug enforcement agency and had infiltrated a conspiracy to export drugs to Scotland. He was an informer, just doing what he was employed by the

Mexican authorities to do. To support his case he had two key witnesses. The first was the man from MI6 who had recruited Marks many years ago to spy on James McCann. He admitted that Marks had been given this role, and that his employment had never been officially terminated. The second was a man the defence brought over from Mexico. He was introduced as an employee of the Mexican anti-drug authority and stated in his evidence that Marks was indeed a colleague, and that his job was so dangerous and secretive that he could not give the jury his real identity.

The jury believed the evidence so skilfully presented, and returned a Not Guilty verdict. Marks was later to admit in his autobiography that the story they had swallowed was indeed a pack of lies.

In many ways these events defined Alan's life. The grass was the straw that broke the camel's back of his marriage. After his release he found it hard to find work, no-one wanting to take on someone with a record for importing drugs. He eventually signed up with Voluntary Service Overseas with whom he worked in several third world countries, where his farming skills and hard work ethic were put to good use. Now in his eighties, he leads a fit and active life, living close to his children and grandchildren.

A few weeks after Alan was arrested, I went back to the house in Glengarry. Jo had asked me to check over the building and pick up a few things for her. I could not resist the temptation to climb up into the attic. It was almost bare. But spread over the floor was what had dropped from the bales as they were being removed. I got a dustpan and brush and filled a bin liner with the sweepings.

When the house had been raided, the bales of grass had been piled high on the gravel at the entrance, from where it had been loaded onto lorries. Thousands of seeds had been dropped onto the ground in the process and the yard was now covered in marijuana plants, each no more than two inches tall. When I returned two weeks later, they had all been carefully removed.

On the way home I stopped at my parents' place in Glencoe and spread the contents of the bin liner over the kitchen table. Ursula was intrigued and insisted I rolled up a bunch of grass into a large joint. I had long ago stopped smoking, Tony was not interested, and so Ursula had the whole thing to herself.

'I just don't understand what all the fuss is about!' she exclaimed with a giggle as she polished and repolished the dish she was cleaning, totally absorbed in her task.

~

For the next few years I continued to work for the Lothian Region Social Work Department. Although employed as a locum, there was plenty of work and most of the jobs were as long-term as I wanted them to be. Occasionally, I would take a break and travel again over the winter, safe in the knowledge that there would be work available on my return.

The winter of 1983 I spent in Sri Lanka. From time to time I would take a bus into Colombo to pick up any poste restante mail, which, if I had any, I would take outside, sit on the steps of the main post office and read in the sunshine. Tony and Ursula had closed the shop for the winter and were exploring rural Shropshire. They wrote from a rented a cottage in Clun that they really liked it there and were looking for a place to retire to. Their business was to be sold.

This meant decision time for me. My lifestyle was enjoyable but not sustainable. I was either going to have to settle into permanent employment with two weeks off a year, retiring at sixty-five with a pension, like most people, or seize this opportunity to do something fundamentally different. I knew that for Tony and Ursula the business had been a semi-retirement hobby. They closed every lunchtime to walk their dogs. It was seasonal, only operating from April to October. They had one part-time staff member. It suited them fine. A new road about to be built would take traffic slightly further away from the business. It was a risk I was prepared to take. I came back from Sri Lanka and put the Buccleuch Place flat on the market. Edinburgh property prices had rocketed and the profit on the flat covered the difference in what the bank would lend and the asking price of the business. In the autumn of 1983, Crafts and Things became mine.

That winter I divided my life between Edinburgh and Glencoe. Monday to Friday I did my social work job, packing up late on Friday afternoons and driving in my ancient VW Beetle up to Glencoe, where I would fit the shop out with wood I had scrounged from Edinburgh skips. My appalling carpentry I covered with brown hessian, but as Tony and Ursula had removed all their antique furniture from the shop I had to make do with what I could afford. I worked to the wee hours of Saturday mornings, grabbed a few hours' sleep, before heading up to my weekend job as a lift attendant at the Glencoe Ski Centre. I worked there all day Saturday, went back to fit out the shop at night, returned up to the ski tow on Sunday and drove straight back to Edinburgh after work to start being a social worker again on the Monday morning. By the spring I was finally able to pack in both jobs to open the business and live permanently in Glencoe. I employed one person part-time but mostly manned the shop on my own, doing the paperwork in the evenings.

Before the end of the decade I had married Kshema, and together we had two sons, built a coffee shop and developed the business. To be around my growing children was of fundamental importance to me, especially after my own experience of a father who was emotionally and frequently physically absent.

We travelled as a family, taking the boys when they were very little to South America for a couple of months of our winter, where with the help of friends we travelled the southern reaches of Chile and Patagonia. Some years later, I walked around a mountain called Kailash in a remote corner of Tibet, one of the highest, loneliest, most desolate and beautiful spots on earth. A place revered by three of the world's major religions. A thin place, like Iona, where my story began.

Acknowledgements

The cover image, *Buachaille, Late Autumn, First Snow*, is reproduced with the kind permission of the artist, John Harris.

The quotations from 'Howl' on page 99 and from 'Mind Breaths' on page 101 are © Allen Ginsberg, reproduced with the kind permission of the Estate of Allen Ginsberg.

'Nobody's Got Any Money in the Summer' written by Roy Harper is used with the kind permission of Carlin Music Corps.

To Rory MacLean for his novel *Magic Bus* which brought back the memories.

To the friends and family who encouraged me to write them down.

To the wonderful staff at Crafts & Things whose hard work freed me up timewise.

To the strangers in foreign lands who showed me kindness and hospitality.

To Jennie Renton of Main Point Books for her practical skills in book production.

To Megan Reid for her editing input.

To you all I would like to say a heartfelt thank you.